Sharika Devi
A Yoginī of Kashmir

शक्त्युल्लासः

Śaktyullāsaḥ

Sharika Devi

A Yoginī of Kashmir

A Volume of Tribute on her Birth Centenary

Edited by
Neerja Mattoo

With an Introduction by
Bettina Sharada Bäumer

DK
PRINTWORLD
Publishers of Indian Traditions

Cataloging in Publication Data — DK
[Courtesy: D.K. Agencies (P) Ltd. <domcinfo@dkagencies.com>]

Śaktyullāsaḥ = Śaktyullāsaḥ : Sharika Devi, a yoginī of Kashmir: a volume of tribute of her birth centenary/ edited by Neerja Mattoo; with an introduction by Bettina Sharada Bäumer.
p. cm.
Includes poems in Kashmiri (Devanagari and roman); with English translation.
Includes bibliographical references (p.).
ISBN 13: 9788124607183

1. Śārikā Devī, 1913-1991. 2. Śārikā Devī, 1913-1991 — Friends and associates. 3. Yoginīs — India — Jammu and Kashmir — Biography. I. Śārikā Devī, 1913-1991. II. Mattoo, Neerja.

DDC 294.5092 23

ISBN 13: 978-81-246-0718-3

First published in India in 2013

Printed and published by:
D.K. Printworld (P) Ltd.
Regd. Office : *'Vedasri,'* F-395, Sudarshan Park
(Metro Station: Ramesh Nagar)
New Delhi – 110 015.
Phones : (011) 2545 3975, 2546 6019; *Fax* : 2546 5926
e-mail : indology@dkprintworld.com
Web : www.dkprintworld.com

Foreword

Prabha Devi

Śrī guruve namaḥ
durgārūpāyai śrī Śarikā devye namo namaḥ

THERE is hardly a Kashmiri who is not familiar with the name of Sharika Devi, who justified and fulfilled the glory of her apt name. An account of her life is contained in the earlier published booklet, *Bhāvārcana* (in Hindi). Here I will try to shed some light on the special attributes of her personality, which was a personification of simplicity.

Always absorbed in spiritual practice, she was mostly reticent, uttering few words. She never faltered in the service of her guru, while keeping a distance from fellow devotees. With her relatives too she maintained only a minimal relationship. Among her other qualities was the perfection with which she performed her own personal chores.

It is Shri Gurudeva himself who correctly evaluated the extraordinariness of her nature and bestowed the title of *Brahmavādinī* on her. Knowing her to be a true devotee, he always treated her with respect and benevolence.

On the eleventh day of her ascent to heaven in 1991, Gurudeva recited the following *mantra*, which he composed in her honour:

Oṁ parabhairava-līnībhūtā ātmaśaktiḥ Śrī Śārikā devī
Oṁ parabhairavalīnyai parāśaktyai Śrī Śarikā devyai namo namaḥ |

One must remember that Gurudeva too left his mortal body within six months after her, the same year. This goes to prove that after her departure, Gurudeva did not think it worthwhile to stay on in this world.

The great scholar from Mithilā, Acharya Rameshwar Jha has this to say about Devi Sharikaji:

Tvam devī nityam Hariparvatasya janasya durgati hari ca durgā |
Kāśmīrikī tvam tanu śāradāsi, kṣīre vasanti śubhadā bhavānī | |

I am proud of the fact that I am the younger sister and a pupil of the Yoginī Devījī. To me my Gurudeva was Lord Śaṅkara and my mother-like elder sister, Devījī none other than Sharika Herself. No matter what I say, it will never be enough to fully describe her many-splendoured personality which was complete in itself. An ideal disciple, constantly absorbed in God-consciousness while never shirking her worldly duties, she was a true devotee. She dedicated her whole life to the service of her Gurudeva with single-minded devotion. I conclude with bowing my head before her pure feet and offering hundred salutations to her and Gurudeva.

I am happy that this volume is being brought out at the centenary celebrations of Sharika Devi. Bettina Bäumer, whom we know as Sharada, has written the Introduction and supervised its publication. May Gurudeva's blessings be with her, always. Along with her, I give my heartfelt blessings to Neerja Mattoo, the editor, who spent valuable time in translating Devījī's poems from Kashmiri, and the contributions which were originally in Hindi. May Gurudeva keep inspiring her too to carry on such valuable work.

Contents

Acknowledgement

I am deeply grateful to Sushree Prabha Deviji for being the spirit behind this book. Not only are the glimpses of Sharika Deviji's wit and wisdom entirely due to Prabha Deviji's having faithfully recorded them, but it is also due to her painstakingly noting them down that Sharika Deviji's mystic Vākhs are being published for the first time.

I am indebted to Sushree Bettina Sharada Bäumer for writing an illuminating, scholarly introduction to the book and also for graciously supervising the work. Thanks are also due to Prof. Sudheer Sopory for taking personal interest in the publication of this book. Finally, I also thank all the contributors for their tributes.

Sharika Devi
An Introduction

Bettina Sharada Bäumer

icchāśaktir umā kumārī
— *Śivasūtra* I.13

SHARIKA Devi is best known as the chief disciple of her great Master, Swami Lakshman Joo, who sometimes said that she was the only disciple to receive full enlightenment from him. Her role as a disciple has been brought out to a certain extent in the volume on Swami Lakshman Joo.[1] But now that her own birth centenary is being celebrated it is also fitting to throw more light on her person and her spiritual achievement — certainly never separate from that of her Master.

Approaching Sharika Devi and trying to make her accessible to those who have not known her requires a fine-tuning to the subtle level of consciousness that was hers. Silence would be a better way of approaching her presence, but words are necessary to communicate her being. In this introduction I intend to try to understand her in the light of the tradition which she embodied, which for lack of a more appropriate name we still call (non-dualist) Kashmir Śaivism.

1 *Saṃvidullāsaḥ: Manifestation of Divine Consciousness: Swami Lakshman Joo, Saint-Scholar of Kashmir Śaivism*, ed. Sarla Kumar and Bettina Bäumer, New Delhi: D.K. Printworld, 2007, 2nd edn., 2010. The two books are complementary. See also the Hindi biography *Bhāvārcana* by Prabha Devi, Srinagar: Ishvar Ashram, 1998.

This introduction is going to proceed in three steps:

1. Her place in the *yoginī* tradition, or the female lineage;
2. understanding her in the light of the great insights of the philosophy and spirituality of "Kashmir Śaivism", and
3. the content of the present volume.

Sharika Devi in the Light of the Yoginī Tradition of Kashmir

There is no doubt that Sharika Devi can rightly be called a *yoginī* who, since her early childhood, was solely devoted to realization of the Divine. *Yoginī*s have, in the Śaiva as well as Buddhist traditions, two apparently contrary natures. On the one hand they are feared as powerful semi-divine female spirits who can create obstacles or even destroy.[2] But the original meaning is that of an accomplished female practitioner, corresponding to the male *siddha*. In the Śaiva context they are described as women "who are ever in union with Śiva".[3] They are not only united with the Divine for their own sake, they help the bound souls (*paśu*) to attain union with Śiva through three kinds of *yoga*.[4] These *yoginī*s can help the souls because they are completely pure and one with the Supreme Lord and are never separated from him.[5] Kṣemarāja explains this permanent union of the *yoginī*s thus:

---

[2] Cf., for example, the chapter on *yoginī* in *Netra Tantra* (chap. 20). Here it is made clear that they destroy only in order to liberate the *paśu*s.

[3] Cf. *Yoginīhṛdaya*, commentary 9 on II.17: *yoginyaḥ, yoga sambandho nityaḥ vidyate . . .*

[4] *Netra Tantra* 20.9-10.

[5] *. . . nirmalā vigataklamāḥ | ekībhāvam anuprāpya na viyuktaḥ kathaṁcana |* — *Netra Tantra* 20.12-13.

> They are completely united, which means they are absorbed (in Śiva), and due to their attaining the supreme bliss they have overcome the impurity based on the wrong identification with the body, the vital energy, etc. hence they are inseparable from Śiva.[6]

A commentary on *Parātrīśikā Tantra* says similarly that "being born from a *yoginī*" (*Parātrīśikā* verse 10) means "attaining the predominance of pure consciousness by reducing the false ego identified with the body".[7]

How fitting is this description of the *yoginī* to Sharika Devi! Her purity, her constant immersion in Śiva (*samāveśa*), and her freedom from the false identity of the ego with the body, making her egoless and transparent to the Divine. And again, she did not consider these qualities as her own possession, but shared them with others, becoming an instrument of grace for others.

Her Master used to call Deviji *brahmavādinī* (a woman sage who has a perfect knowledge of the Absolute) in most of the letters written to her.[8] Even more than that, Swamiji often addressed her as *jīvanmuktā* (one liberated while alive), the highest confirmation of her supreme state.

The tradition of Kashmir Śaivism has a clear lineage of *yoginīs*, starting from Ardhatryambakā, the daughter of Tryambaka, the founder of the non-dual Śaivism. Abhinavagupta calls this separate lineage "well-established".[9]

---

6 Commentary on *NT*, vol. II, p. 220, 2012-13.

7 *Parātrīśikā Vivṛti* by Lakṣmīrāma on verse 10.

8 *Brahmavādinī* is a concept from the Upaniṣads and it does not occur in the Āgamas or in the Śaiva literature. It stresses the aspect of divine knowledge.

9 *Tantrāloka* 36.13: *sa cārdhatryambakābhikhyaḥ saṁtānaḥ supratiṣṭhitaḥ*. Jayaratha precises that the two non-dualist traditions are Trika and Kula.

We do not possess many witnesses of this female lineage. But Abhinavagupta quotes occasionally with great respect brief sayings of three *yoginīs*: Keyūravatī, Madanikā and Kalyāṇikā. Keyūravatī was a female Guru in the lineage of Jñānanetra of the Krama tradition,[10] but unfortunately no work has come down to us in her name or in the name of the other *yoginīs*. But it is certain that she bestowed initiation on female disciples.[11]

Even if we lack texts and historical evidence, there is no doubt that these female lineages continued in their own and yet powerful way. It is only centuries later that we meet the great women saint-poets, foremost of all Lallā or Lāl Dêd in the fourteenth century. She is the most well-known and influential female saint of Kashmir, honoured and quoted by all sections of society, irrespective of their religious belonging. This is not the place for a comparison (which would be in any case impossible), but the achievement of Sharika Devi and Lallā meets in the mystical experience, based on *kuṇḍalinī yoga*, and transcending all dualities. The famous and frequently quoted Vākh of Lallā could be equally applied to Devī Śārikā:

My Guru gave me only one advice:
from outside turn your gaze within.
That became my initiation:
Thus I began to dance naked.[12]

"Naked" is surely not to be understood literally, but in the sense of being free from the bonds imposed by society.[13]

What is common to both is the state of introvertedness,

---

[10] Cf. A. Sanderson, *The Śaiva Exegesis of Kashmir*, p. 275.

[11] A. Sanderson dates these *yoginīs* between CE 875–925 (ibid., p. 411).

[12] Vākh 94 in Grierson.

[13] Similarly "dancing" refers to an ecstatic state, called *ghūrni* by Abhinavagupta, reeling under the impact of bliss.

which was a permanent spiritual state of Deviji (*antarmukhatā*). One important difference in the lives of the two saints is that Sharika refused to get married and enjoyed the state of a *brahmacāriṇī*,[14] whereas Lallā had to pass through the ordeal imposed on her by her husband and mother-in-law, before she could free herself completely.

Many of the Vākhs of Lallā could also be an expression of Deviji's experience, such as:

Deeds I performed became an offering
Words I spoke became mantra
Experiences my body had were for self-knowledge
This is the essence of the path of Śiva Tantras.[15]

Another outstanding example of a woman saint-poet is Rupa Bhavani in the seventeenth-eighteenth century, who attained the heights of mystical experience, and whose spiritual influence is still alive among Kashmiri Pandits. Her mystic poetry also shows the spirit of non-dual Śaivism and of the *kuṇḍalinī* experience. Her poetic expression is equally powerful. To give only one example:

The one who meditates and consciously weighs oneself,
Judges none and is judged not,
Only waits for Him and His benediction,
Such a one will fuse with the Eternal One.
— tr. Neerja Mattoo

These are only some well-known examples for the *yoginī* tradition which Sharika Devi continued in her own way. The thread running through such different female saints is a non-dual mysticism, the importance of the Guru, and the stages of *kuṇḍalinī yoga* leading to a transcendent state beyond dualities.

---

14 The letter of the young Lakshman Joo, addressed to her father, defending her from getting married, has become famous.

15 Vākh 70 in Jaishree Kak Odin, *To the Other Shore: Lalla's Life and Poetry*, p. 137.

Sharika Devi: An Embodiment of the Philosophy of Kashmir Śaivism

This leads directly to the important question how Sharika Devi embodied the great insights and ideals of Trika and Pratyabhijñā in her life and experience. We have the scriptures on the one side and the lived experience on the other, and the important point is the connection between the two. Sharika Devi was well-versed in the Śāstras, she had studied Sanskrit and learnt, together with her sister Prabha, the important texts of the tradition from Swami Lakshman Joo. She never showed off her knowledge which could only be guessed from occasional remarks she made while studying the texts. She could well have taught them herself but she humbly submitted herself to her Guru's teaching.

But the correspondences I want to point out between the teachings and her life are not based on any conscious effort, they are the spontaneous outflow of her spiritual state. "Spontaneity" could be another translation of *svātantrya*. All the more one can say that her life — as the life of her Gurudeva — was itself a commentary on the teachings of the tradition.

Among the central concepts what comes first to mind is Śakti, in relation to Śiva. It is Deviji who gave the title Īśvara Svarūpa to her Master, but if he was perceived as Bhairava, she was Śakti, the gentle and yet powerful energy on his side, inseparable and yet distinct.

A poet compared Swamiji to a mighty *cināra* tree, but I would compare Deviji to a *śirīṣa* tree, whose red flowers are extremely delicate and full of nectar, but which has strong roots. Two *sūtra*s of the *Śiva-Sūtra*s come to mind: *gurur upāyaḥ*, (the Guru is the means) (II.6), and *icchāśaktir umā kumārī* (the divine energy of volition is Umā, the virgin) (I.13). The various interpretations Kṣemarāja gives of the latter *sūtra* are perfectly fitting to Sharika Devi. Not only was she a virgin "who remained in a state of subject and never became an object enjoyed by others", she had perfectly united her will to the Divine as embodied in her Master. The energies of cognition and activity (*jñāna-śakti* and *kriyā-śakti*) emerge only from the primary (and hence virgin) energy of Will.[16] Paradoxically it is the total surrender of her will to the Master which gave her the power to be herself. And this is the characteristic of the *śāmbhava* state, the highest, divine state of *samāveśa*, depending solely on Will. In the meaning of the *sūtra* relating to the penance of Umā, Swamiji summarizes the commentary of Kṣemarāja thus:

> At the time when Umā was virgin, she was completely detached from the world of enjoyment. When she had given herself to perform penance in order to receive the blessing of Lord Śiva, her mind was one-pointedly focused only on Lord Śiva. She was always one with that being of Śiva. In the same way, the desire of such a *yogī* is completely one-pointed. He always wills entry in his own nature and nothing else.[17]

At the human level of the relationship of guru and disciple, the disciple is called *dūtī*, the spiritual companion of the perfect Master or *siddha*. This relationship can take different forms, but in the case of Swamiji and Deviji it was of a purely spiritual nature.

In her spirituality, Sharika Devi embodied the ideals of introvertedness (*antarmukhatā*), from which she was never distracted; one-pointedness towards her divine goal; and being ever established in her own nature of supreme I-consciousness: *akr̥trima ahaṁbhāva*. The adjective *akr̥trima* is

---

[16] A. Sanderson translates it as "pre-cognitive impulse", because it is not "will" directed to an object.

[17] *Śiva Sūtras, The Supreme Awakening*, revealed by Swami Lakshman Joo, New Delhi: Munshiram Manoharlal, 2007.

so fitting because everything in her was natural (literally "non-artificial"). It was her naturalness which at the same time hid her true nature from the insensitive observer. It could be called her humility, but not in any artificial sense. In the face of so much of artificiality and self-conceit found in so-called spiritual circles, her example shines as the embodiment of authenticity.

Closer to the religious traditions of Kashmir, she was true to her name. Her parents had a deep relationship with the Sharika Devī Rock and Temple, and her guru saw in her an embodiment of the Sharika Devī of Hariparvat. The great Pandit Acharya Rameshwar Jha of Banaras also celebrated her as a living incarnation of the presiding goddesses of Kashmir: Śārikā, Śāradā, Kṣīrabhavānī Durgā.[18] As described in *Samvidullāsaḥ* (p. 180), on the day of Deviji's departure from the *āśrama* on her final journey, a few days before her *samādhi*, Swamiji held a mirror before her and asked her to have a *darśana* of the Devi — before she closed her eyes.

More in a joking mood, but yet in a very fitting comparison, Swami Lakshman Joo himself compared the three ashramites of Ishvar Ashram to the Trika of Śiva, Śakti, Nara: Evidently he himself was Śiva, Deviji being Śakti, and Prabha Deviji completing the trinity in the way of Nara.

Coming back to Deviji's spiritual experience I only want to give an example of her very subtle and mystical insights. Utpaladeva's *Śivastotrāvalī* was one of the favourite texts of both, guru and disciples. It is difficult to fathom the level of experience which these mystical verses evoked in them. But Swamiji himself told about Deviji experiencing one particular verse which transported her to another level of consciousness:

---

[18] See the *ślokas* on p 12.

vilīyamānāstvayyeva vyomni meghalavā iva |
bhāvā vibhāntu me śaśvatkramanairmalyagāminaḥ ||
— *Śivastotrāvalī* 6.7[19]

In the paraphrase of Swamiji:

> Let me feel this objective world, this universe of objectivity, just like clouds lying in the ether of your consciousness. As there are heaps of clouds in the sky, in the same way let me feel this universe as a mass of clouds in the sky of God-consciousness. Just as the clouds fade by and by and only the blue sky is left afterwards . . . ; in the same way this universe should appear to me, purified and having become one with Thee in the end. Let me feel that way.[20]

This expresses Deviji's universal experience of the Divine.

The Contents of the Volume

The present volume does not pretend to be a biography of the *yoginī*. It is an homage to her continued presence and inspiration, hundred years after her birth, and twenty-two years after her final *samādhi*. It contains her own mystical poems which can be rightly called Vākh, in the tradition of Lāl Dêd. Sharika Devi did not intend to compose poetry, but her inner experience spontaneously poured forth in a very gentle song. Most of these Vākh have been collected by her sister Prabha Devi, whenever she heard them.

---

19 In the translation by Rhodes Bailly:

Just as cloud droplets are absorbed in the sky,
So are the various constituents of the universe
Absorbed in you,
May they always shine visibly for me
As I proceed through the stages of spiritual growth.

20 *Śivastotrāvalī of Utpaladeva: Exposition by Swami Lakshman Joo*, New Delhi: D.K. Printworld, 2008, p. 101.

They express her disillusionment with the world, and her attraction to the Divine, her surrender, and her total dedication. She also reveals the centre of her spiritual practice, which is an overcoming of duality true to the tradition. The basic tone is one of *bhakti*, but not of the ordinary dualistic type. The Tantras themselves extol to practise *parābhakti* which in its intensity transcends all dualities.[21]

All this is paired with a realistic self-reflection and an awareness of her shortcomings. But her dedication and her great love for the Divine is crowned by the ultimate experience of self-recognition (*pratyabhijñā*):

One day I knew who I was . . .
everything I saw as extension of my self

Her vision is purely internal:

With eyes closed, I saw everything . . .

The original Kashmiri is certainly more close to her feelings expressed, but the excellent translation by Neerja Mattoo makes these Vākh come alive for the non-Kashmiri too.

The second section contains reminiscences by Deviji's devotees, disciples and family members, and by some great scholars. She was fully recognized by Ācārya Rameshvar Jha, as shown in the verses quoted in the beginning. These contain elements of her life that can be used for a future biography. But Deviji's life was so straightforward and, externally seen, uneventful: from her childhood to her initiation by her divine Master, to her moving to his *āśrama* to spend the rest of her life in his nearness and in his service. The real biography would have to trace the stages of her spiritual life which was so hidden and maybe known only to her Master. It is such biographies which can inspire and guide seekers for times to come.

---

[21] Cf. *Parātrīśikā Tantra*, verse 33.

The third section contains anecdotes from her life which express her wisdom. They are mainly related to her relation to her guru. Prabha Devi carefully noted down such meaningful events and exchanges between guru and disciple, and we truly get glimpses of the spontaneity of her life and thought. To her, situations of daily life would contain a spiritual message which she was quick to grasp, and to pass on her insights as practical teachings.

These "glimpses" also throw light on the social situation of the *āśrama*, on the different characters of the devotees flocking to the great Master, and on Deviji's understanding of their psychology. Truly in the style of most saints, Deviji uses simple metaphors to drive home a profound truth.

She was suffering most from what she once told me: "people come here for all kinds of selfish purposes, but nobody comes for God".

May this collection of her wisdom inspire the reader to be more intensely engaged in the search of the Divine. It is Sharika Devi's grace that will go a long way to support it.

Śārikā Devī Carcāstavaḥ

Acharya Rameshwar Jha

त्वं सेविता येन हृदा मनोज्ञा ।
ते प्रापि सर्वेश्वरता नृलोके ॥

tvaṁ sevitā yena hṛdā manojñā ।
te prāpi sarveśvaratā nṛloke ॥

(O Sharika Devi!)

The one who worships you with heart and mind,
he attains universal lordship in the world of men.

काश्मीरिकी त्वं ननुशारदासि
क्षीरे वसन्ती शुभदा भवानी
त्वं देवि ! सत्यं हरिपर्वतस्था
जनस्य दुर्गार्तिहरी च दुर्गा ॥

kāśmīrikī tvaṁ nanuśāradāsi
kṣīre vasantī śubhadā bhavānī ।
tvaṁ devi ! satyaṁ hariparvatasthā
janasya durgārtiharī ca durgā ॥

You are the Goddess Śāradā of Kashmir,
Bhavānī, who dwells in the ocean of milk, bestowing blessing.
O Goddess! Durgā truly you are, seated on Hariparvat,
Removing the troubles of people so difficult to overcome.

प्रणम्या सहजानन्दा देवी सा ब्रह्मवादिनी ।
यद् दयादृष्टि पूतोऽहं भ्राजे स्वानन्द निर्भरः ॥

praṇamyā sahajānandā devī sā brahmavādinī |
yad dayādr̥ṣṭi pūta 'haṁ bhrāje svānanda nirbharaḥ ||

Bowing to her, the Goddess full of spontaneous bliss,
The one who proclaims the Absolute (*brahmavādinī*),
Purified am I by her compassionate look
And full of the bliss of the Self am I.

श्रीमती शारिकादेवीं नित्यानुग्रहरूपिणीम् ।
वन्दे नित्यं परां शक्तिं भक्तानुग्रहकारिणीम् ॥

śrīmatī śārikādevīṁ nityānugraharūpiṇīm |
vande nityaṁ parāṁ śaktiṁ bhaktānugrahakāriṇīm ||

I praise the Lady Sharika Devi,
Ever of the nature of grace,
The Supreme Śakti
Bestowing grace on her devotees.

श्री शक्तिं शारिकां नौमि सर्वदां ब्रह्मवादिनीम् ।
स्मरणेनापि यस्यास्तु महामोहः प्रलीयते ॥

śrī śaktiṁ śārikāṁ naumi sarvadāṁ brahmavādinīm |
smaraṇenāpi yasyāstu mahāmohaḥ pralīyate ||

I praise the blessed Śakti Śārikā
Who is ever proclaiming *Brahman.*
By merely remembering her,
Illusion, no matter how great, gets dissolved.

श्री विद्यया पूजित पादुकायै
श्री शंभु सेवार्थ गृहीत कायै ।
रामेश्वरस्याखिल बोध मूर्त्यै
देव्यै नमः ज्ञानद शारिकायै ॥

śrī vidyayā pūjita pādukāyai
śrī śaṁbhu sevārtha gr̥hīta kāyai |
rāmeśvarasyākhila bodha mūrttyai
devyai namaḥ jñānada śārikāyai ||

Homage be to Sharika, the bestower of knowledge,
Whose feet are worshipped through Śrīvidyā,
Who has assumed a body in order to serve Śiva (her Master),
She, the embodiment of enlightenment for Rāmeśvara.

1. Sharika Devi in *samādhi* on her Birthday

2. Marriage of Sri Jawaharlal Sopory with Gunavati, sister of Swami Lakshman Joo. Sharika (ca. 1½ year old)

3. Sharika (ca. 20 years) with her brother Mohanlal (ca. 16 years)

4. Sharika Devi, Swami Lakshman Joo, Prabha Devi, the three ashramites of the upper Ashram (ca. 1960)

5. Deviji at the feet of her Master at the upper Ashram (ca. 1930s)

6. Swamiji's Birthday (ca. 1952)

7. Swamiji giving ṭīkā to Deviji on his Birthday (ca. 1975)

8. Swamiji giving ṭīkā to Prabha Devi on his Birthday (ca. 1978)

9. Deviji in *samādhi* on Swamiji's Birthday (ca. 1978)

10. The Yoginī (ca. 1972)

11. Swamiji and Deviji on their *āsana*
in the veranda of Ishvar Ashram (ca. 1978)

12. Deviji in her own *Svarūpa*

13. Satsang in Ishvar Ashram (1987)

14. The saintly sisters, Ishvar Ashram (1986)

15. *Samādhi* with open eyes

16. Deviji's room with her meditation seat (after her *samādhi* in 1991)

17. The presiding Devī of Ishvar Ashram (1988)

I

सुश्री ब्रह्मवादिनी शारिका देवी जी की कतिपय कश्मीरी भाषा में उच्चारित कविताएं

Sharika Vākh

Mystical Poems of Sharika Devi

1. Brahmā's Gift

ओसुस ना दिगम्बर ब्रह्माहन सूज़नम डॅल्य।
बस्त खलरा गयम नॅल्य ब्रह्माहन सूज़नम डॅल्य॥१॥

पंच़न हुन्द बन्यव चीज़ केंह काल रूदस मीच़।
कालशाहमार गोमा नॅल्य ब्रह्माहन सूज़नम डॅल्य॥२॥

ब्रह्म संज़ यि सृष्टि मायाय मंज़ बस्ती।
कांह ना रूद अमिनिश खॅल्य ब्रह्माहन सूज़नम डॅल्य॥३॥

मायाय पत दोरान ज़्योन मरुन छुन सोरान।
वोन्य ना फेरय ब बॅल्य बॅल्य ब्रह्माहन सूज़नम डॅल्य॥४॥

म्य कम्यूहॅव वथ म्य हा छम गोर संज़ सथ।
ज्ञानॅच्य हॅवनम मशाल्य ब्रह्माहन सूज़नम डॅल्य॥५॥

यूगियन अति मस्ती ज्ञनियन पॅनन्य हस्ती।
आनन्दक्य च्यवान प्यॅल्य ब्रह्माहन सूज़नम डॅल्य॥६॥

osus nā digambar brahmāhan sūẓanam ḍālya ।
basta khalarā gayam nālya brahmāhan sūẓanam ḍālya ॥1॥

pañcan hund banyav cīẓ keṅh kāl rūdas mīc ।
kāla shāhmār gomā nālya brahmāhan sūẓanam ḍālya ॥2॥

brahmā sanẓ yi sṛṣṭī māyāya manẓ bastī ।
kāṅh nā rūd aminiś khālya brahmāhan sūẓanam ḍālya ॥3॥

māyāya pat dorān ẓyon marun chuna sorān ।
vony nā pheray ba bālya bālya brahmāhan sūẓanam ḍālya ॥4॥

mya kamyū hāv vath mya hā cham gor sanẓ sath ।
jñānac hāvnam mashālya brahmāhan sūẓanam ḍālya ॥5॥

yūgiyan ati mastī jñāniyan pānanya hastī ।
ānandakya cyavān pyālya brahmāhan sūẓanam ḍālya ॥6॥

Unclad, a free spirit I was, but Brahmā sent me a gift,
The burden of this human hide, Brahmā sent me this gift.
Of five elements it was fashioned, measured by the yardstick of Time
A deadly serpent took it in its coils, Brahmā sent me his gift.
This creation of Brahmā, this habitation of illusions,
Everyone caught in its embrace, Brahmā sent me this gift.
Chasing a mirage, all thoughts of life and death forgotten!
No more shall I wander aimless, Brahmā sent me this gift.
Who showed me the true path? The guru is the one I trust,
He lighted the torch of Knowledge, Brahmā sent me this gift.
The *yogīs* are intoxicated, the learned in their own identity,
Drinking cups of distilled joy, Brahmā sent me this gift.

2. Śyāmsundara

तोहि मा ढ्यूठवोन शामसोन्दरय
तोहि मा ढ्यूठवोन शामसोन्दरय।
युसहय न्यबर सुय मन्य अंदरय
तोहि मा ढ्यूठवोन शामसोन्दरय॥१॥

व्रच़् म्यान्यि गूपिय न्यूख छ़्लरॅविथ
दूरान दूर्यव घर बार त्रॅविथ।
घर छिस सरिय छुस न कुन्य घरय
तोहि मा ढ्यूठवोन शामसोन्दरय॥२॥

अथि छस मोरली नॅल्य पीतांबर
च़्न्च़्ल नेथॅर नाव मुरलीधर।
मुरली सॅत्यन मुहरावनय
तोहि मा ढ्यूठवोन शामसोन्दरय॥३॥

दिवकी वसुदीव प्राणापानय
दिह म्योन आसवुन छुय जेलखानय।
मध्यस मंज़ ज़ाव कृष्ण गोन्दरय
तोहि मा ढ्यूठवोन शामसोन्दरय॥४॥

tohi mā ḍhyūṭhvon śāma sondaray
tohi mā ḍhyūṭhvon śāma sondaray |
yus hay nyabar suy manya andaray
tohi mā ḍhyūṭhvon śāma sondaray ||1||

vrac myānyi gūpiya nyūkh chalarāvith
dūrān dūryav ghara bār trāvith |
ghara chis sariy chus na kuny gharay
tohi mā ḍhyūṭhvon śāma sondaray ||2||

athi chas morli nālya pītāṁbar
cañcal nethār nāv muralīdhar |
muralī sūtyan muhrāvanay
tohi mā ḍhyūṭhvon śāma sondaray ||3||

divakī vasudīv prāṇāpānay
dih myon āsvun chuy jelakhānay |
madhyas maṅẓ ẓāv kr̥ṣṇa gondaray
tohi mā ḍhyūṭhvon śāma sondaray ||4||

Did you see Him anywhere, my beautiful Śyām?

The One out there, but at once within the heart,

Did you see Him anywhere, my beautiful Śyām?

Oh those *gopīs*, who tricked Him away,

Far far away He went, leaving homes empty,

But does He really have a home, my beautiful Śyām?

A flute in hand, dressed in yellow, his teasing eyes,

His name Muralīdhar, casts a spell with his flute,

Did you see Him anywhere, my beautiful Śyām?

Devakī and Vasudeva — *prāṇa* and *apāna* (inhaling and exhaling breaths)

In my body, a prison house in which was born the bonny Kṛṣṇa!

Did anyone spot my beautiful Śyām?

3. I Am That, That Is Me

ज़ागि रोज़हा पन्यपानस ज़ागि रोज़नस छुम न वार।
काम, क्रूध मोह ब्ययि अहंकार ज़न त दोरान गुरि सवार॥
माजि मायाय हुन्द यि व्यवहार अनज़ानन प्यठ प्रहार।
शक्तिपातच्य त्रावत नज़राह ज़ागि रोज़नस यीयि म्या वार॥१॥

ज़ागि रूज़िथ खुलि म्य च्योन द्वार अद अच़् च्योन दरबार।
तति वज़ान बाजि ब्यय सेतार ज़ीवस खसान पोज़ खुमार॥
न छु बाजि तय न छु सेतार च़ीतनच्य छय यि तार।
सुय छुस बय, बय छुस सुय तति प्यवान सोर संसार॥२॥

दिह अभिमानुक छु क्या ज़ोर जल लगान बरसॅय छु तोर।
राज़ बनिथय दिह भाव सोस नाव प्यवान छुस ज़ीव बिचोर॥
यलि फेरि पोत ब्ययि वाति तोत तीज़ सुय तेल्यस च़्वपॅरय।
ज़ागि रोज़ह दुरदानस ज़ागि रोज़नस छुम न वार॥३॥

ẓāgi roẓahā panya pānas ẓāgi roẓnas chum na vār ।
kām, krūdh moh byayi ahaṁkār ẓan ta dorān guri savār ।।
maji māyāy hund yi vyavhār anẓānan pyaṭh prahār ।
śaktipātacy trāv ta naẓarāh ẓāgi roẓnas yīyi myā vār ।।1।।

ẓāgi rūẓith khuli mya cyon dvār ada aca cyon darbār ।
tati vaẓān bāji byay setār ẓīvas khasān poẓ khumār ।।
na chu bāji tay na chu setār cītanacya chay yi tār ।
suy chus bay, bay chus suy tati pyavān sor saṁsār ।।2।।

dih abhimānuk chu kyā ẓor jal lagān barsāy chu tor ।
rāẓ banithay dih bhāv sos nāv pyavān chus ẓīv bicor ।।
yali pheri pot byayi vāti tot tīẓ suy telyas cvapāray ।
ẓāgī roẓaha durdānas ẓāgi roẓnas chum na vār ।।3।।

I would fain lie in wait, but Ah, my inability to do so!

Desire, Anger, Attachment and Ego, like horsemen they chase me.

The mother we love, but others we assault

Let Your Grace fall on me, O Lord, so that I could lie in wait,

If I could only do that, Your doors would open for me to enter.

The music of the instruments that resounds there, truly intoxicates one.

No instruments but the strings of consciousness resonate.

I am That, That is me — the material world falls away,

Pride in the body only shuts those doors to one

A king you feel and the body-consciousness drops away,

Otherwise only a pathetic being you are.

If you look back to where you came from,

A dazzling light will shine all around.

I would fain lie in wait for the Beautiful One, but Ah, my inability to do so!

4. My only Desire

द्वयी हुन्द गाश वॅन्य सोरॅयोम
च़्यत-प्रकाश अद त्येल्योम।
म्य गरि गरि ॲस यहोय अभिलाष
म्य नो संसारचय कांह आश॥१॥

करय सुबह शाम अर्च़न च़्य
करय गरि गरि अर्च़न बय।
च़ हावतम वोन्य पननुय गाश
म्य नो संसारचय कांह आश॥२॥

च़ मन कॅसि हंज़ म थव वोन्य आश
यि संसार नो थवान कांह बाश।
यित गछ़ छुय यत्युक सारांश
म्य नो संसारचय कांह आश॥३॥

dvayī hund gāsh vānya soryom
cyat-prakāś ada tyelyom |
mya gari gari ās yahoy abhilāṣ
mya no saṁsārcay kāṅh āś |1|

karay subah śāma arcan cya
karay gari gari arcan bay |
ca hāvtam vonya pananuy gāś
mya no saṁsāracay kāṅh āś ||2||

ca mana kāsi haṅẓ ma thav vonya āś
yi saṁsār no thavān kāṅh bāś |
yita gach chuy yatyuk sārāṅś
mya no saṁsaracay kāṅh āś ||3||

The light of duality fades away
The radiance of self-awareness dazzles forth
This was my one desire, all the time —
That I have no hope from the world.
Morning and evening I make offerings to You
Make offerings to You, again and again,
That Your light shine upon me now,
So I have no hope from the world.
Trust no one else, Oh my mind,
The world leaves you bereft,
The cycle of birth and death, that is its only essence,
I have no hope from the world.

5. Samadṛṣṭi

दोह म्य गोमो सोंबरान त रछ़रान
तोति भास्योम नोखसान।
हा ज़ीवो वुछू च़ यकसान
अद ना छुय चे़ नोखसान॥

doh mya gomo soṁbarān ta racharān
toti bhāsyom nokhasān |
hā ẓivo vuchū ca yaksān
ada nā chuy ce nokhasān ||

My days go in gathering and preserving,
But still I have nothing to show but loss.
Cast the same look at everyone, everything,
Then there will be no sense of loss.

6. Know the Centre

द्वयी हुन्द परॅद च़ठ रोज़ खबरदार
प्राणापानुक मध्य च़य ज़ान।
यहोय गव भक्तिभाव यहोय गव ध्यान
दोन हुन्द मध्य ज़ानुन गव श्राण॥

dvayī hund parād caṭh roẓ khabardār
prāṇāpānuk madhya cay ẓān ।
yahoy gav bhakti bhāv yāhoy gav dhyān
don hund madhya ẓānun gav śrāṇ ॥

Tear away the curtain of duality,

Know the centre of *prāṇa* and *apāna*.

That is your *bhakti*, that your meditation,

Know the centre of the two — that is the Truth.

7. Śaraṇam

शिवस शरण गछ़ शिवस शरण गछ़।
शिवस शरण गछ़ शिवस शरण गछ़।
च़लिय यि त्यलि खुर शिवस शरण गछ़।
शिवस शरण गछ़, शिवस शरण गछ़॥

च़्य काम क्रूधुक कोरूथ यि व्यवहार
च़्य नो यि ज़ोनुथ अपुज छु संसार।
छयोनुय म तोल यति च़ नेरख
शिवस शरण गछ़ शिवस शरण गछ़॥

यि छयम म्य बॅरया यि छुम म्य सन्तान,
हतो च़ ज़ीवो म कर यि अभिमान।
चन्दस छयनिस प्यठ गछ़ख परेशान
शिवस शरण गछ़ शिवस शरण गछ़॥

वछुथ च़्य फिरथुर अमी चे़ ओय खुर
म वुछ प्रमेयस च़ रोज़ प्रमाता।
च़लिय यि त्यलि खुर, शिवस शरण गछ़
शिवस शरण गछ़ शिवस शरण गछ़॥

अन्दर च़्य गर्भस कोरूथ यि वादय
दोहस त रातस ब यूग साधय
च़ प्योख थन यलि मोठुय च़्य सोरूय
शिवस शरण गछ़ शिवस शरण गछ़॥

दितुय यि धोखय च़्य लूभ मूहन
अमृत पुत्रो यि छुय न शूभन।
व्यकास चोनुय च़ क्याज़ि लूभन
शिवस शरण गछ़, शिवस शरण गछ़॥

śivas śaraṇ gach śivas śaraṇ gach ।
śivas śaraṇ gach śivas śaraṇ gach ।
caliy yi tyali khur śivas śaraṇ gach ।
śivas śaraṇ gach śivas śaraṇ gach ॥

cya kāma krūdhuk korūth yi vyavahār ।
cya no yi ẓonuth apuj chuz saṁsār ।
chyonuy ma tol yati ca nerakh ।
śivas śaraṇ gach śivas śaraṇ gach ॥

yi chyam mya bārayā yi chum mya santān,
hato ca ẓīvo ma kar yi abhimān ।
candas chyanis pyath gachakh pareśān ।
śivas śaraṇ gach śivas śaraṇ gach ॥

vvchuth cya phirathur amī ce oy khur
ma vuch prameyas ca roẓ pramātā ।
caliy ye tyali khur, śivas śaraṇ gach
śivas śaraṇ gach śivas śaraṇ gach ॥

andar cya garbhas korūth yi vāday
dohas ta rātas ba yūga sādhay ।
ca pyokh thana yali moṭhuy cya soruy
śivas śaraṇ gach śivas śaraṇ gach ॥

dituy yi dhokhay cya lūbh mūhan
amr̥ta putro yi chuy na śūbhan ।
vyakāsa conuy ca kyāẓi lūbhan ।
śivas śaraṇ gach śivas śaraṇ gach ॥

Seek refuge in Śiva, in Śiva seek refuge
The tangles will untangle, in Śiva seek refuge.
Trading in Lust and Anger, you never knew,
The world is illusion. Deluding with false weights,
Deluded yourself, empty-handed you are.
"This my wife, this my son", an empty boast!
Stripped of possessions, seek refuge in Śiva.
Upheavals you saw, hence the confusion.
Do not look at objects, Be the Subject yourself
And all enigmas will be resolved at once,
Seek refuge in Śiva, in Śiva seek refuge.
In the womb you made a pledge,
That you would fix your mind on Him, day and night,
But once born, the pledge and all the vows you forgot,
Seek refuge in Śiva, in Śiva seek refuge.
Deceived you were by greed and attachment,
Does it behove one who was born from *amṛta*?
One who was destined to rise, must not fall prey to delusion.
Seek refuge in Śiva, in Śiva seek refuge.

8. Remember Your True Identity

जाय चॅन्य छय शमशान बल पनन्य हन्य मॅव ज़ाह डल।
संसार युथना करी छ़ल तस हंज़्य गन्यराव कल॥

यतिना छु कँसि रोज़ुन ती ना तोग कँसि बोज़ुन।
मायायि कोरनय यि छ़ल पनन्य हन्य मव ज़ाह डल॥

jāy cānya chay śamśān bal pananya hanya māv ẓāh ḍal ।
saṁsār yuthnā kari chal tas haṅẓya ganyarāv kal ॥

yatinā chu kaṅsi roẓun tī nā tog kaṅsi boẓun ।
māyāyi kornay yi chal pananya hanya mav ẓāh ḍal ॥

Your ultimate destiny is the cremation ground

Do not forget your true identity.

Let not the world deceive, fix your mind only upon Him.

No one will stay for ever, this fact no one remembers,

Illusions play this trick — never forget your true identity.

9. The Temple of the Body

यि मंदर म्योन छु क्याह शूभिदार
बिहिथ अथ मंज़ छु बोड सरकार।
दिमस यलि वन्य वुछ्यन यकबार
यि मंदर म्योन छु क्याह शूभिदार॥१॥

छि आसवन्य अथ दोगुण पंच् द्वार
कहिम मन दीव पारुद ह्यू
दवान ओर योर करान हू हू
छु संसारुक यि नज़दीक यार।
यि मंदर म्योन छु क्याह शूभिदार॥२॥

yi maṁdar myon chu kyāh śūbhidār
bihith atha maṁẓ chu boḍ sarkār ।
dimas yali vanya vuchyan yakbār
yi maṁdar myon chu kyāh śūbhidār ॥

chi āsavanya atha doguṇ pañca dvār
kahim mana dīva pārud hyū
davān ora yor karān hū hū
chu saṁsāruk yi naẓdīk yār ।
yi maṁdar myon chu kyāh śūbhidār ॥

What a grand edifice my temple is!
Seated within is the Highest Lord
Whenever I look for Him, He is there to behold,
What a grand edifice my temple is!
Twice five doors, ten apertures in all, it has,
The mind, restless like quicksilver,
Darts this way and that, crying in confusion
Forges a foolish bond with the world!
What a grand edifice my temple is!

10. Parābhakti

दिह अभिमानुक पाप छुमा मनसय
मत दूरतम छुम च्योनुय राग।
यित निश निश आनन्द बनि मनसय
गरि गरि थावतम पननी ज़ान॥

ज़ान्य प्यठ रूज़िथ वातॅ च्योन दरबार
अद ना छम कँसि हंज़ ति यति लार।
लारान लारान वातॅ च्योन दरबार
मत दूरतम छुम च्योनुय राग॥

dih abhimānuk pāp chumā manasay |
mata dūrtam chum cyonuy rāg ||
yit niś niś ānanda bani manasay |
gari gari thāvtam pananī ẓān ||

ẓanya pyaṭh rūẓith vātā cyon darbār |
ada nā cham kaṅsi haṅẓ ti yati lār ||
lārān lārān vātā cyon darbār |
mata dūrtam chum cyonuy rāg ||

My mind, tainted with sin — pride in the body,
Please do not distance Yourself, I love you so!
Come close and fill me with bliss,
Let me not know anyone but You for ever!
Fixed upon You, I will reach Your abode,
And never have to heed any other call.
Only to You would I come on this chase,
Please do not distance Yourself, I love You so!

11. Old Age Approaching

यि कुस आव यि कुस आव वार वार आव।
लोत लोत आव नरयन जंगन जुव ज़न द्राव॥
यि कुस आव यि कुस आव॥१॥

अछ्यव ह्योत वुछुन कम कनव ह्योत बोज़ुन कम।
दंद कतारन अल ह्यू च़ाव,
यि कुस आव यि कुस आव॥२॥

बब लालस वथरुन त्राव
पतकञि गाव तकिया थाव।
अरिस कमरस डॅख ह्यू च़ाव,
यि कुस आव यि कुस आव॥३॥

नाव छुम बुजर पत्यमिस ग्राव,
मॉली करान पोशन क्राव
अड्यन च़टान अड्य अत्य थाव
यि कुस आव यि कुस आव॥४॥

बुजर वुछिथॅय अल ह्यु च़ाव
गछ़नुक वॅन्य समया आव
लठस दह गज़ वलिथय द्राव
यि कुस आव यि कुस आव॥५॥

yi kus āv yi kus āv vār vār āv |
lot lot āv naryan jaṅgan juv ẓan drāv
yi kus āv yi kus āv ||1||

achyav hyot vuchun kam kanav hyot boẓun kam |
daṅd katāran ala hyu cāv
yi kus āv yi kus āv ||2||

bab lālas vatharun trāv
patakañi gav takiyā thāv |
aris kamaras dakh hyuv cāv
yi kus āv yi kus āv ||3||

nāv chum bujar patyamis grāv
mālī karān pośan krāv |
aḍyan caṭān aḍya atya thāv
yi kus āv yi kus āv ||4||

bujar vuchithāy ala hyu cāv gacha nuk vānya samayā āv |
laṭhas dah gaẓ valithay drāv
yi kus āv yi kus āv ||5||

Who is it that comes with such slow steps,
Stealthily he creeps in, and life oozes out of the limbs?
Who is it that comes, who indeed?
The eyes grow dim, hearing is faint,
The rows of teeth begin to shake,
Who is it that comes, who indeed?
Make a bed for the old man, he needs a bolster,
His back, once so straight, is bent like a bow.
Who is it that comes, who indeed?
My name is Old Age, he says, a regret for the past,
The gardener plucks some, leaves some on the plant.
Who is it that comes, who indeed?
The sight of this visitor sets one atremble,
The time to leave has come, one knows,
The time to wrap oneself in a length of cotton cloth.
Who is it that comes, who indeed?

12. Nothing but All-pervading Bliss

गफलथ गयम गफलथ गयम,
गफलथ गयम गफलथ गयम।
ॲसी म्य स्वर्गक्य जाम नॅल्य
कामन–त क्रूधन करिम ॲल्य,
यिम जाम भीद गगरव खेयम
गफलथ गयम गफलथ गयम॥१॥

गफलथ छू ज़ीव भावुक चिह्न,
गफलथ छु वासनाय हुन्द प्रेयम।
गफलथ यहय वतिथ प्ययम
गफलथ गयम गफलथ गयम॥२॥

ज़ीवो क्षण क्षण बुध च़ रोज़
अद बोज़ख अन्दरिम च़ सोज़।
सोज़स मंज़य न्यन्दर प्ययम
गफलथ गयम गफलथ गयम॥३॥

धारान धोरुम सकल रूप,
मॅशिरोवुम पननुय सु रूप।
काल शक्ति वतिथ प्ययम
गफलथ गयम गफलथ गयम॥४॥

संसार निश यलि पत्य ब च़ास
केंह काल कोरुम ईकान्तवास।
तत्त्वशक्ति वॅतिथ प्ययम
गफलथ गयम गफलथ गयम॥५॥

दोह अकि च़्यूनुम छुस ब कुस
सत्‌चि़त आनन्द रूप युस।
विषयन हंज़य नफरथ गयम
नफरथ गयम नफरथ गयम॥६॥

शक्तिपातच यलि प्रव प्यमम
सोरुय वुछुम पननुय स्वभास
हिय थॅर ज़न फोलिथय ब आस
यति प्यठ ब ऑस तमिकुय यि भास
सोरूय वुछुम पननुय व्यकास
अद कालसॅय गव अति ग्रास
सोरूय वुछुम पननुय व्यकास
सोरूय वुछुम आनन्द व्यकास॥७॥

gaphalath gayam gaphalath gayam ।
gaphalath gayam gaphalath gayam ॥
āsi mya svargakya jām nālya
kāman ta krūdhan karim ālya ॥
yim jām bhīd gagarav kheyam ।
gaphalath gayam gaphalath gayam ॥1॥

gaphalath chū ẓīv bhāvuk cihn ।
gaphalath chu vāsanāya hund preyam ।
gaphalath yahay vatith pyayam ।
gaphalath gayam gaphalath gayam ॥2॥

ẓīvo kṣaṇ kṣaṇ budh ca roẓ ।
ada boẓakh andarim ca soẓ ॥
soẓas mañẓay nyandar pyayam ।
gaphalath gayam gaphalath gayam ॥3॥

dhārān dhorum sakal rūp
māshirovum pananuy su rūp
kāl śakti vatith pyayam
gaphalath gayam gaphalath gayam ॥4॥

saṁsār niś yali patya ba cās
keṅh kāl korum īkāntavās |
tattva śakti vatith pyayam
gaphalath gayam gaphalath gayam ||5||

doh aki cyūnum chus ba kus |
sat cit ānanda rūp yus ||
viṣayan haṅẓay napharath gayam |
napharath gayam napharath gayam ||6||

śakti pātach yali prav pyayam
soruy vuchum pananuy svabhās
hiya thār ẓan pholithay ba ās
yati pyaṭha ba ās tamikuy yi bhās
soruy vuchum pananuy vyakās
ada kāl say gav ati grās
soruy vuchum pananuy vyakās
soruy vuchum ānanda vyakās ||7||

Oh what a mistake I made, a blunder it was!
I was dressed in heavenly robes,
The moths of desire and anger made them their nest
Holes were bored in them by the rats of duality.
What a mistake I made, what a blunder it was!
Errors define the human condition,
Error lies in attachment to sin
This was the error that visited me,
What a mistake I made, a blunder it was.
Be aware, all the time, and you will hear
The inner music of the soul.
But in the midst of its resonance, I fell asleep.
A mistake I made, what a blunder it was!
But once I assumed a universal form through meditation
No longer aware of my individual self,
The Cosmic power was before me, all of a sudden!
A mistake I made, what a blunder it was!
When I renounced the world and
Entered a state of seclusion,
Full knowledge of things stood before me.
A mistake I made, what a blunder it was.
One day I knew who I was,
One bathed in the light of *sat-cit-ānanda*
In disgust I turned away from desires,

Turned away in disgust,
When the benediction of *śaktipāta* I felt
The whole world seemed a reflection of my own self.
Like a honeysuckle vine I bloomed,
Everything bore an imprint of where I had come from
Everything I saw as extension of my self,
Then it was that Time itself was vanquished,
Everything I saw as extension of myself.
Everywhere I saw nothing but all-pervading bliss.

13. The Lord of my Heart

च़्यत दीव म्योन क्या छु नुन्दबोन आसवुन।
प्रथ दीवस त ज़ीवस मंज़ छु बासवुन॥

मायायि मंज़ रूज़िथ छुय न्यरमाय।
भीद भावच अख ज़र छस ना ग्राय॥

पॅन्य पानय छु पानस ज़ाग्य आसवुन।
च़्यत दीव म्योन क्या छु नुन्दबोन आसवुन॥

रुप-रंग रोस चे़ननुय ओत छु आसवुन।
तथ्य मंज़ छुय ब्योन ह्यू ज़न त भासवुन॥

हंग मंग छुय पनुन रूप खटिथ थाववुन।
च़्यत दीव म्योन क्या छु नुन्दबोन आसवुन॥

cyat dīv myon kyā chu nundabon āsavun ।
pratha dīvas ta ẓīvas maṅẓ chu bāsavun ॥

māyāyi maṅẓ rūẓith chuy nyaramāy ।
bhīda bhāvaca akh ẓar chas na grāy ॥

pānya pānay chu pānas ẓāgya āsavun ।
cyat dīv myon kyāh chu nundabon āsavun ॥

rūp raṅg ros cenanuy ot chu āsavun ।
tathya maṅẓ chuy byon hyu ẓan ta bhāsvun ॥

haṅg maṅg chuy panun rūp khaṭith thāvavun ।
cyat dīv myon kyā chu nundabon āsavun ॥

How beautiful the Lord of my mind and heart is,
In every mortal or god He is to be seen.
Seated in the material, yet unattached He is.
Not the faintest trace of duality in His bearing,
Himself the Watchman to His own Self!
How beautiful the Lord of my mind and heart is!
Formless and colourless, He can only be felt,
As a separate, unique, omnipresence,
Though He hides His beautiful face for no reason!
How beautiful the Lord of my mind and heart is!

14. My Eyes found Light

न छुम मानुक म्य कांह अभिलाष
न छ्यम संसार चय कांह आश।
अन्यन अछिनय म्य आमो गाश
म्यनो संसार चय कांह आश॥१॥

गज़ल खानन ब वुज़नॅवनस
अज़ल नामय म्य लेखन आव।
यिमन अछिनय म्य आमो गाश
म्य नो संसारचय कांह आश॥२॥

na chum mānuk mya kāṅh abhilāṣ
na chyam saṁsār cay kāṅh āś ।
anyan achinay mya āmo gāś
mya no saṁsār cay kāṅh āś ॥1॥

gazal khānan ba vuzanāvnas
azal nāmay mya lekhan āv ।
yiman achinay mya āmo gāś
mya no saṁsār cay kāṅh āś ॥2॥

Neither desire for honour have I,

Nor any expectations from the world!

My sightless eyes are blessed with light,

Nothing I desire now from the world.

The Divine Singer woke me up

And my destiny was written down.

My eyes found light, why should I look to the material world?

15. Freedom From Desires

संसार छुय मुह जंजाल वासना गाल वासना गाल।
अॅस वहरिथ छु काल शाहमार वासना गाल वासना गाल॥

वासना छय शोंगिथ शाहमार वासना ज़न त यच़कोल ब्यमार।
विषयन वुछिथ गछान हुशयार वासना गाल वासना गाल॥

अज्ञानॅच छि गॅज्य वुहवुञ काम क्रूध पाकॅनावान।
भूगान छु तथ ज़ीव कंगाल वासना गाल वासना गाल॥

बाज़-गशॅ फेर शिव-भाव प्राव सोरुय ज़गथ म्य मंज़ द्राव।
प्रथमाभासॅ परज़नाव लाल वासना गाल वासना गाल॥

अॅथ्य थानस वनान छि शमशान अति रोज़ान पान भगवान्।
दीह गॅलिथ भस्मा मोच़ान वासना गाल वासना गाल॥

अति नो रोज़ान छि छ़ल बल अति नो रूद कामुक बल।
अॅथ्य ज़ागि रोज़ रोज़ि नो काल वासना गाल वासना गाल॥

विषयव सूॅत्य मेलि नो दय नज़ि बनि अमि सॅत्य पापन क्षय।
यि छि सॉरय वासनायि हंज़ चाल वासना गाल वासना गाल॥

saṁsār chuy muha jañjāl vāsanā gāl vāsanā gāl |
ās vaharith chu kāl shāhmār vāsanā gāl vāsanā gāl ||

vāsanā chay shoṅgith shāhmār vāsanā ẓan ta yacakol byamār |
viṣayan vuchith gachān huśyār vāsanā gāl vasanā gāl ||

agyāñca chi gājya vuhvuñ kām krūdh pākanāvān |
bhūgān chu tath ẓīv kaṅgāl vāsanā gāl vāsanā gāl ||

bāẓ gasha pher śiva bhāv prāv soruy ẓagath mya maṅẓ drāv |
prathamābhās paraẓanāv lāl vāsanā gāl vāsanā gāl ||

athya thānas vanān chi śmaśān ati roẓān pāna bhagavān |
dīh gālith bhasmā mocān vāsanā gāl vāsanā gāl ||

ati no roẓān chi chal bal ati no rūd kāmuk bal |
athya ẓāgi roẓ roẓi no kāl vāsanā gāl vāsanā gāl ||

viṣayav sūtya meli no day naẓi bani ami satya pāpan kṣaya |
yi chi sāray vāsanāyi haṅẓ cāl vāsanā gāl vāsanā gāl ||

The world is a snare of attachments, kill your desires, do.
With mouth open, the death-python lies in wait,
Kill your desires, do.
Desires are a sleeping dragon, desires are a long-ill invalid,
Who wake up at slght of materials enjoyable —
Kill your desires, do.
The hearth of ignorance forever blazing,
Over which the pot of lust and wrath simmers,
Which the beggared Betng relishes.
Kill your desires, do.
Turn away and Find Shiva consciousness
From which the whole world emanates,
Know the Truth in the first light, at first sight,
Kill your desires, do,
That state is known as the cremation ground,
Where God Himself resides,
Material and sensual dissolves, ashes remain.
Kill your desires, do.
No deceit, no pretence, lust falls, defeated,
Wait for the Grace, Death will be vanquished,
Kill your desires, do.
Physical senses cannot apprehend God,
Nor will sins be washed through them,
It is all a trap of desire,
Kill your desires, do.

अन्तिम आत्म-कथा
देवी जी के शब्दों में

Antim ātma kathā

Devijī sandyan laphẓon mang

Seeing with Eyes Closed

क्याह कर बॅर छस गॅमच़् बर द्रायस न ज़ांह।
कल नॅमिरिथ रूजुस दोहय कल तुलुम न जांह॥

ॲछ वटिथ वुछूम सोरूय ॲछ वाहरय़म न ज़ांह।
हिरन संदि पॅठ्य रूज़्ॅस वनन छ़ाल मारय़म न ज़ांह॥

नाफ़् आसुम अन्दरय मुशुख आयम न्यबॅरय।
तीर ह्यथ लारेयम पतय अथि आयस न ज़ांह॥

kyāh kar bar chas gamac bar drāyas na ẓāṅh ।
kal namirith rūjus dohay kal tulum na ẓāṅh ॥

acha vaṭith vuchūm sorūy acha vāharyam na ẓāṅh ।
hiran sandi paṭhya rūẓās vanan chāl māryam na ẓāṅh ॥

nāph āsum andaray mushukh āyam nyabāray ।
tīr hyath lāreyam patay athi āyas na ẓāṅh ॥

Deviji's last words — a summary of her life:

Ah! A tree bereft am I, never stepped out of the threshold,

My head I kept bowed always, never raised it at all.

With eyes closed, saw everything, never opened them at all.

Like a deer, the forest was my abode, but never bounded or frolicked in it.

The musk was within me, but its scent burst out, never contained.

With a bow and arrow they chased me, but never could they grasp my essence.

II
Tributes and Reminiscences

The Making of a Yoginī[1]

Mohan Lal Sopory

I REALLY consider myself very fortunate that I remained associated with Sri 108 Swami Ishvar Svarup, Swami Lakshman Joo. Swamiji's elder sister Gunawati, was married to my respected elder brother, Jawaharlalji. Therefore there was a great deal of amity between the two families. Once Swamiji remarked:

> When I entered this house for the first time with my sister, I perceived the presence of a particular person with whom I had been closely associated in my last life. But I did not reveal this knowledge to anybody. Suddenly, one day a young girl appeared before me and the old remembrance returned as if a certain recognition occurred.

This young girl was my elder sister Sushri Sharika Devi who had a saintly disposition from childhood. Often when we played together, she would mould a Śivaliṅga out of mud. She would enjoy worshipping it or she would write *Rāma Rāma* on paper for the whole day and then consign it to a river. This was for her play as a child, which continued for many years. After some years it was destined that a *haṭha-yoga* ascetic came to our house. Our father welcomed him and gave him the

[1] Reprinted with kind permission of the editors from: *Samvidullāsaḥ: Manifestation of Divine Consciousness, Swami Lakshman Joo, Saint–Scholar of Kashmir Śaivism*, ed. Bettina Bäumer and Sarla Kumar, New Delhi: D.K. Printworld, 2007, pp. 155-59.

facility of staying with us. Sharika Devi learnt the technique of *prāṇāyāma* from him. In a short while she started experiencing absorption in the Self. One day Swamiji Mahārāja came to our house and discerned her state of inner contemplation. He gave me the following command:

> Bring her to me. I will resolve many of the knots in the path of Yoga. She will thus gain mastery in the practice of Yoga.

I was still a child and replied simply, "Mahārāj, our parents will be unhappy". Swamiji said that through his blessing I would not experience any impediment. Even if I came at night I would not be beset by dogs or thieves, nor would my parents raise any objection. I accepted his order and thus Sharika and I started going to Swamiji.

This was Sharika Devi's first attempt to go to Swamiji. At this time Sharika would accompany me to Swamiji and would learn Sanskrit grammar, meditation, etc. from him from 4 a.m. to 9 a.m. and I would proceed to school and later to college in pursuit of my education. One day Swamiji said to me, "You and I will camp at the beautiful spot called Gopītīrtha, near Nishat for a few days". Swamiji had taught me the technique of meditation while I was still a child. I felt very happy with the prospect. Through Gurudeva's inspiration Sharika Devi, my younger sister Prabhaji and my nephew Motilal also came there after some time. They were accompanied by Swami Muktananda.[2] After a few days Sharika Devi said to Swamiji, "Grant me the state whereby I can attain my true divine nature". It was 6 o'clock in the evening. Swamiji was seated on a deck chair. He said, "The vision of the Supreme within the self comes only with intense meditation and relinquishment of worldly desires. I am an ordinary person. How can I grant

---

[2] Not to be confused with Swami Muktananda of Ganeshpuri who came much later to Swamiji.

your wish?" Deviji was adamant. She said, "You are the embodiment of Lord Śiva. I am certain that you have the power to do so. My unflinching devotion will finally make you relent." After uttering these words a flood of tears started to flow and continued till 12 o'clock at night. Muktanandaji was watching this scene. Both the children (Prabhaji and Motilal) were sleeping, Swamiji instructed me to take them and lay them under the *cināra* tree outside. Seeing the unabated torrent of tears of Sharikaji Muktananda said to Swamiji, "Are you intent on killing this girl? There is a law governing the relationship between the devotee and the Lord." This spectacle appeared to be one where a child was insisting on getting the moon. Muktanandaji went out of the tent. I was watching the awesome divine play with folded hands. After 12 o'clock Swamiji appeared as Lord Śiva Himself. He said to Deviji, "Come before me and recite the *Śivastotrāvalī* worshipping me as Lord Śiva". Deviji did so for one hour, weeping continuously. It was 4 o'clock when Swamiji placed his right hand on her head. With the touch of Swamiji's hand, Devi's tears dried up and she was lost in herself for twenty minutes. After this she said to Swamiji, "I am now experiencing the fullsome state of *samādhi*, replete with divine fragrance". Swamiji understood her state of complete spiritual fulfilment. He said: "Now you can ask for all the boons you want and I will grant them". She begged that she should remain celibate and always immersed in meditation. These two wishes she asked very happily but was hesitant to ask for the third, but Swamiji persuaded her to ask for that also. Thus she had no option but to ask for her third boon wherein she wished that she and the Master would stay together for ever. Then Swamiji said, *tathāstu* (let it be so) and her three prayers were granted.

By this time dawn was about to break. Mahārājajī took Deviji to a nearby stream which was full of water. He unrobed her and bathed her there with his own hands. Then he washed her face and put on her clothes. We were strolling near the stream. Deviji, while chewing a tooth pick gazed at Swamiji and said: "I am truly manifest in every atom. Your power is pervading everywhere. I can give salvation to Mohan Lal". Swamiji was listening to every word silently. By this time they had reached the tent. He said: "The time is not yet ripe for you to remain in this state. There are still many tasks for you in this world. When the time comes I will restore your original state." After ages, it is only the very fortunate who know such spiritual states. Those who witness these are indeed blessed.

Swamiji was now silent and Deviji, who began experiencing the objective world again was in tears. She implored her Master to restore her divine state. It seemed as if the moon had lost its power to cool or a snake had been deprived of its gem.[3] When Deviji found that her state of complete fullness and bliss would not be recovered, she became almost mad. She could not see with one eye and developed low fever. Seeing her in this condition, Swamiji considered it best to send her home. We quickly breakfasted and packed, asking Muktanandaji and the two children to return home separately. The three of us hired a *tonga* (horse cart). Swamiji sat in front while Sharika Devi and I sat at the back. By the time the *tonga* reached opposite Nehru Park, Deviji abused Swamiji. He turned to look upon Sharika and I felt as if I had the *darśana* of Lord Śiva. I presume that Deviji saw the manifestation of Lord Śiva in all His glory in Swamiji. She now begged for forgiveness in all humility. After some time we reached the city and dropped Swamiji at his residence in Fatehkadal. Then Sharika and I proceeded to our residence in Sarafkadal.

Our parents were upset when they saw Deviji who was

---

[3] In Hindu mythology the cobra has a gem in its hood.

sick. They laid her on a bed and after a couple of days her condition worsened. They called the famous doctor Dinanath Ganju. He saw her and said that the girl could not survive beyond a few days. After this he left. In the meantime my mother sent me to Swamiji. Deviji was experiencing the last states of life.

When I arrived at Swamiji's residence he said, "When you return from college bring a quarter kilo of grapes". When I returned at 4 o'clock I gave the grapes to Swamiji who picked just three grapes and said: "Put these in Sharikaji's mouth, one by one". A miracle occurred when she ate the grapes. She opened her eyes, stretched herself and started looking all round, whereas, previously she could not even drink water.

This was the glory of Swamiji Lakshman Joo who was no ordinary *yogī* but a *yogīrāja* who had achieved yogic powers even as a child. He had a unique technique of meditation whereby he could interact in the objective world while he remained absorbed in the Self. He was in contact with people yet he was aloof. Swamiji was truly an exceptional scholar who knew all the subtleties of Śaiva Śāstras and above all he was a phenomenal Gurudeva who transcended all conceptions of a renunciate.

In the days to come two beautiful houses were built on the Ishvar hill near Nishat by the respective parents of these two great souls. I had started going to college. Mahārājajī was very fond of me and wanted me to stay with him but my mother pleaded with him and said: "O Lord how can I see both my children renounce the world?" Then Swamiji answered: "Very well! You can get Mohan Lal married. He will remain devoted to me even while he is a family man."

One day I went to Swamiji and he took me for a boat ride in the Dal Lake. When the boat reached the middle of the lake, suddenly a cyclonic wind arose. The boat became unsteady and people on the shore feared that it would capsize. Swamiji asked me and the boatman to close our eyes for five minutes. He forbade the boatman from plying the oars. Thus the three of us sat motionless. Suddenly the rain and storm abated and after some time we came ashore. Such was the supernatural, divine power of Swami Lakshman Joo.[4]

I was studying in college. One day Swamiji said, "You have a few holidays, so let us go to Draphama, which is beyond Harvan and the hunting ground of kings". I gladly accepted Swamiji's command and reached Swamiji's residence on the following day. We had taken a bag of rice, a mud pot and some salt from Harvan. We walked for several hours and reached a spot called "Darvanya". Swamiji said: "We will rest here and then make arrangements for meal". I collected some small dry twigs and made a cooking oven with stones, Swamiji lit the fire and he placed the earthenware pot with some water and rice on the fire. We used a stick instead of a ladle. He added a little salt and soon the rice was ready. He covered the rice and placed it on coals. Then he went to the stream with pure bubbling water. The forest was very dense. We had no plates for serving the rice. I was watching this *līlā* (divine play) amazingly. Swamiji got two stones from the water and served the rice on them asking me to start eating. We were hungry and enjoyed the meal. We had some cold water and then sat on a mat under a tree. We could hear the roaring of wild animals and the chirping of birds all around us. I felt very frightened. Swamiji lit a fire.

"Now no wild animal will attack you. You can meditate without any anxiety." I sat in front of the fire till twelve at night, Swamiji was immersed in *samādhi*. At dawn we bathed and returned home. Every action of our Gurudeva was replete with divinity.

[4] Compare the stilling of the storm by Jesus, Mark 4.35-41.

Once, when I was still a child I visited Swamiji's house with Deviji. He said: "I will take Sharikaji to Hariparvat at night". I did not accompany them. Swamiji tied a turban on Sharika's head and took her to Hariparvat disguised as a boy. When they returned home in the morning Sharika Devi said to me:

> I had a vision of all the gods and even the seven sages appeared to me. All the rocks at Hariparvat are manifestations of various gods. It is for this reason that it is considered a sacred place where all one's wishes are granted.

Thereafter I too visited Hariparvat off and on.

When the old memories surge up in the mind I am carried to a splendid world of beatitude. Thus I experienced many wonderful events. Whenever I met my Master he looked upon me with the same compassion and love that I had known as a child. In 1991 when he returned from America he had become physically very weak. My heart sank. Understanding my state he reassured me that he was in a divine blissful state of mind and that it was only natural that the body lost its vitality at the end of life.

Words cannot describe the glory of our Gurudeva. My entire life was filled with his grace. I make this offering of adoration at his holy feet.

Homage to Sharika Devi*

Prithvinath Pushp

A LOTUS leaf swims in water, but never gets wet, never lets a drop of water rest on it, never absorbs it in itself. It is unique, unattached, never dry or parched, but smooth, pure and moist. It is not prickly, but soft, not lax or enervated, but firm.

A similar uniqueness was the characteristic trait of the Śaiva devotee Sharikaji. While always busy with her routine, she was so accessible — a living spirit that was naturally established in the highest state of *sādhanā*. Existing at a plane where she was both within the world and beyond it at the same time, she had achieved that ideal balance and become its most trusted symbol. The harshest storm or worst turbulence would not make the flame of her gentle, collected smile flicker. She never kept anything for herself, but was a free-flowing stream of energy that illuminated with a dazzling light all who stood within her grace. The resident deity of Ishvar Ashram! To a *yoginī* of her stature, who, even after attaining *nirvāṇa* continues to be an invincible source of inspiration, my salutations.

* Translated from the origenal Hindi by Neerja Mattoo.

Vision of Calmness*

B.N. Pandit

A PERSON goes through many different experiences in life; some are pleasant, some are bitter. This happens particularly when many disciples live together under the tutelage of a guru. This is a situation similar to where students, studying under a competent teacher, driven by a desire to go ahead of the fellow students, sometimes even resort to hatching little plots to undermine rivals. . . .

Even though living in an atmosphere of such competitiveness, even jealousies, for years, Devi Sharikaji never allowed these to come in the way of her spiritual journey, nor did her devotion and service to the guru suffer any permanent damage. In fact, she continued to have compassion for all those women who were jealous of her. Even a spiritually evolved, *siddha yogī* can feel hurts, but he or she does not let these affect his or her inner self. Deviji lived a similar kind of life, but with her spiritual strength and detachment, she did not allow such negative feelings to reside in her mind. With a mind free from rancour, she was busy in serving her guru, day and night, devotedly. This is her exceptional *tapasyā*, the fruit of which was to be seen by all when she left her physical body. Gurudeva showed deep respect and affection for her. Other women disciples mutely saw this with their own eyes. . . .

---

* Excerpts from a tribute in Hindi, translated by Neerja Mattoo.

How carefully and strictly, according to the principles of Śaivism, Gurudeva arranged her funeral and performed her last rites himself. He declared that the place where she was cremated, be considered a holy place (*tapobhūmi*) and not used for any material purpose. His instructions and conduct prove the high esteem in which Swamiji held Devi Sharikaji. All the petty attempts made by new women disciples to cause her pain during her lifetime, were forgotten, as though her passing away had disarmed them to the extent that they were totally forgotten.

The behaviour of evolved beings and true seekers is beyond the comprehension of ordinary people. Deviji understood this truth very well and thus she never complained. Whatever was Gurudeva's decision, she accepted it without any questioning. Whenever Gurudeva asked for her opinion on a matter, she would give it in clear terms, without mincing words. She never compromised with the truth, irrespective of whether Gurudeva accepted her opinion or not.

I cannot express in words my deep feeling of reverence for Deviji. All I can say is that whenever I saw her gentle, calm face I would be reminded of her Paramaguru Swami Mahtabjoo's countenance, gentle, calm and totally at peace. The very sight of such faces gives rise to an exceptional sense of peace in the beholder and I was fortunate to be one of those privileged beholders.

Sharika Devi
Stable in Supreme Conscious State

Kapil Sopory

REVERED Sharika Deviji — Didda Pyariji (beloved elder sister) — remains in our memory as an epitome of highest level of spirituality with the least show-off and an exterior image of a commoner with nothing to boast of. She would carry out all her divine duties towards her guru most compassionately but with due eagerness and extreme devotion.

Being my father's younger sister, me and other youngsters in the family had regular social contacts where she would be met as a religious super power for whom we all had highest regard. Her approach used to be of an elderly respected householder. Beyond this, I failed to benefit from her highest level of spiritual knowledge. It was provided by and by, and much later by her younger sister, Prabhaji, called Behen Pyariji in the family, who was my Hindi tutor for long. We could read Didda Pyariji's verses which used to be jotted down by Behen Pyariji when those were being recited while carrying out various chores. Brief but crisp and deeply meaningful, they reflect the Truth one needs to understand via one's own inner core.

In my childhood, I learnt the way she came across her guru, who was brother of my father's first wife (he had remarried after the great lady's soul left the world). My family members — my father particularly — were not in favour of this closeness of a young girl with one who had renounced worldly pleasures and remained a *brahmacārī* (celebate) throughout. When the family was planning to marry her off to a well-placed young man, he was compelled to refuse on the ground that Didda Pyariji had appeared in his dream as a Devi and warned him not to think of the marriage.

On realizing that Didda Pyariji was not meant for a worldly life, her father built for her a house in close vicinity of her guru's house where she resided for long and got complete training and knowledge of Śaiva scriptures. Thus developed her spiritual personality further and fully.

When our family left the Valley for plains in 1947, Didda Pyariji and her Gurudeva were part of the group. We went to many places where we lived like wanderers without a definite future plan. The religious and spiritual pursuits of the two continued however.

Back to the Valley, Gurudeva shifted to a new abode where Didda Pyariji also came to live. They lived there throughout their bodily existence on this universe.

Didda Pyariji was *mauna* (silence) personified. She spoke less and only what was necessary, shunned publicity of any sort and preferred to remain in solitude. I have made some analysis of why she would have preferred *mauna*. May be, because:

- the journey towards the ultimate aim of life begins with *mauna*,
- *mauna* leads to union with the Almighty,
- *mauna* leads to differentiation between bodily and real Self-experience,
- *mauna* brings forth the fructified power to concentrate on the Universal Consciousness.

Didda Pyariji well understood that man is able to express

his feelings and thoughts. But when he is unable to express them, he desires to express himself through silence. She well understood and did express mildly that all feelings, thoughts, speech and silence are just to indicate that there is something wonderful within us that feels good, listening about which, thinking about which and experiencing which we feel good. She subtly wished ignorance within us to perish so that eternal truth is established.

Such has been our Didda Pyariji. She continues to shine brightly and exude her godly fragrance around us. There are occasions when we celebrate in her honour to let everyone gain spiritually by reviving the remembrance specially and bowing affectionately before her.

May her grace be always on us!

From Darkness to Sunshine

Suresh Sopory

FROM the lush green Himalayas, snow-clad mountains, the valley in the wilderness, solitude lover Divine Soul made Her base with Śaiva Ācārya Guru Swami Lakshman Joo Mahārāj. Her father, Pandit Jialal Sopory housed his daughter in the vicinity of the habitation (*āśrama*) of Swami Lakshman Joo Mahārāj renowned in the Valley amongst his devotees and others as a descendant of Lord Śiva and known as Īśvara Svarūpa. From her early adolescence Sharikaji was accepted by Guru Īśvara Svarūpa who bestowed upon her the enormous knowledge of Śaivism. This knowledge was keenly grasped by His devotee Sharikaji; the guru knew the devotional attainment within Deviji which made her the foremost top devotee of Guru Mahārāj.

It was in later years that Deviji's sister, Prabhaji also joined the core with her as per the consent of the Master to give her place to become part of Ishvar Ashram for all times to come. The morning rising sun beyond the high mountains, chirping of birds, hundreds of trees and beautifully coloured flowers made Ishvar Ashram with its two devotees a heavenly abode. Sharika Devi never expressed openly the tremendous philosophical knowledge of Śaivism. We were part of the discourses by the guru on various Sundays. The discourses would commence by chanting of *śloka*s by Prabha Devi. Sharika Devi would also be there in deep silence, closed eyes, realizing within herself the guru and almighty Lord Śiva. Devotees used to come from the downtown of the Valley to the *āśrama* to have *darśana* of the guru and Sharika Devi.

In those days I happened to visit the *āśrama* once in a while and made myself comfortable at the back of the hall. I sat with my eyes closed and concentrated on Deviji. The dreaming impression of Deviji made me chant, "Sharika, Sharika, Sharika". I don't remember what made me a devotee of Sharikaji within a flash of my chanting. I opened my eyes and found that Deviji was looking at me as if her *dr̥ṣṭi* fell on me, this was a turning point of my career and I achieved everything which I have, only by her blessings on me.

I consider myself to be a pebble in the list of her devotees. Both the sisters stayed for a short spell of time in our house in Kingsway Camp area of Delhi. I was sitting at her feet once and I requested her something for my salvation for whole life. She with her inner sense immediately bestowed on me her divinity and that is still with me till date and will remain unto my last breath. There are many incidences in my life whereby the mere chanting of Deviji's name changes the entire course of motion of the river of life. The mind, body and soul have to be concentrated for self-realization, which she taught me. She said, "Time is no concern, place is no concern, direction does not matter for chanting guru's name". All these embedded thoughts have made a deep impression in the retina of the eye. To me she is alive with me all the time showering blessings. Where Deviji a devotee of guru in the true sense and Lord Śiva, left for her heavenly abode. I happened to be in Nilokheṛī. On receiving this (unexpected) news I sent a telegram saying, *"brahmavādinī ātmaśaktaye"*. This was probably not understood by anyone there. When I reached Jammu personally, I showed this written on a wooden plank to Prabhaji, who took me to Īśvara Svarūpa. Guruji was taking a separate room ironing his clothes. Guruji kept the plank on a towel and taking a deep breath and concentrated. Then suddenly he said, "Let's go down to the garden".

A table was brought, a towel was spread, the plank was kept on it and garlanded by Guruji. A video was shot. Guruji told me this needs to be further purified. On his command the next morning I sat with Guruji and he composed two *śloka*s on Deviji:

> *parabhairava līnībhūtā ātmaśaktiḥ śrīśārikādevī,*
> *parabhairava līnyai parāśaktyai śrī śārikā devyai namo namaḥ.*

Guruji has given me his hand-written manuscript saying: *gas ye thav panas nish* (keep this with you).

Devi Sharikaji is an answer to the link between Īśvara Svarūpa, Lord Śiva and her entire devotee's world. Everyone who reads this article is requested to chant "Sharikaji Sharikaji" with full devotion and see the results for themselves.

Deviji is always within us, will remain to the end of this world. As a blessing of Swamiji, Devijis traditon is continued by Devi Prabhaji everyday, month by month, year by year. We all owe everything to her now as to Devi Sharikaji.

The Divine Mother

Subodh Sopory

ON the eve of the auspicious centenary celebration of Shri Sharikaji (Didda Pyariji), I thought of writing a few instances, which have remained in the back of my mind since long, depicting the power of words spoken by Shri Sharikaji, which to me were real miracles.

I was born in the Sopory's house at "23, Wazir Bagh, Srinagar", which had all the blessings of the three great ones of Ishvar Ashram, Nishat, namely Swami Lakshman Joo (Īśvara Svarūpa), Sharikaji (Didda Pyariji) and Prabhaji (Behen Pyariji).

My childhood was spent in a religious atmosphere and the effect of saints and their presence gave me wisdom, innocence and purity. I still try to maintain the discipline inculcated since then.

I recall an instance when I was studying in Amar Singh College, Srinagar. Our examinations were going on. Sharikaji came to our house and stayed for the night. Next morning I went to her before going to the college. She asked me, "which paper is today?" I told her, "it's mathematics". She told me, "in today's paper you will come first". I never took it seriously, as frankly speaking, I never came first earlier. But when the result of this paper was announced, I was surprised that I secured the highest marks in the class. These were her powers and blessings.

I recall another instance, way back in January 1969, when Srinagar was reeling under extreme cold, and all road and air travel was blocked. On one such a day, I got a telegram from Oil and Natural Gas Commission (ONGC), Dehra Dun, asking me to appear for an interview. I was having only one day in between and to go to Dehra Dun seemed impossible. Incidentally, the day I got the telegram it was Wednesday when Īśvara Svarūpa, Didda Pyariji and Behen Pyariji would visit our house. Mohan Lal (Bhai Pyareji) told me to wait for Īśvara Svarūpa and his advice. They came around 11 a.m. After bowing at their feet, my mother told Sharikaji about my interview. She paused for a moment and said "Subodh will attend this interview". She then turned towards Swamiji. Bhai Pyare apprised about the weather conditions and Īśvara Svarūpa said: "Book his ticket by air to Amritsar, from there he can go to Dehra Dun".

Tickets were booked for the 12:30 p.m. flight next day. On the day of departure, the sky was overcast and I was thinking how would I go. I was looking at the sky and at 11:30 a.m. the clouds were getting cleared as if they were making path for an aircraft. The flight took off in time and I reached Amritsar. From there I reached Dehra Dun at 7 a.m. on the interview day. When I reached my maternal uncle's house I found in the newspaper there the headline: "Heavy snowfall in Kashmir, Valley cut off from rest of country". My uncle was surprised to find me there and asked me how did I reach there? I said: "It is because of Didda Pyariji's words that I have to attend this interview." I got selected and spent all my career with ONGC till my superannuation.

During my career, I had spent many years in Vadodara. In mid-1980s Didda Pyariji and Behen Pyariji visited our place. We were so blessed with their presence. The day they arrived, Didda Pyariji told me in the evening to book their return ticket for a date after twelve days. To get a confirmed ticket was not possible those days at a short notice. I asked her that if it is not available can I get on for some other day? She with a smile told me, "you will get it for this day only". When I gave the reservation form, the railway clerk out of curiosity asked me, how did you know that two seats are available for this day, otherwise, we do not have any seats even after one month. I was taken aback. It was a miracle. When I reached home, she gave a very pleasant smile and asked whether I got the tickets. I said yes. The next sentence was: "These I had already arranged".

One day Didda Pyariji expressed her desire to see the sea. Because of time constraint, it was not possible to go to Mumbai from Baroda, so we all went to the nearest sea shore at Bay of Khambat, Cambay, which is facing the Arabian Sea. She and Behen Pyariji were so delighted to be there. It was a first time experience. I told them that on their next visit we will go to Mumbai, but that never happened.

On way back I took them to ONGC's drilling site. On seeing the huge drilling rig (the machine used for drilling earth for producing oil) she got scared and told me that you leave this job. I explained her everything and she blessed me but in her heart of heart I could feel she was slightly disturbed and was reluctant to take food that night. She was so kind, generous and compassionate, and had feeling for one and all.

After Didda Pyariji left her body in 1991, once Prabhaji came to Mumbai and spent some memorable days with us. The day she was to catch a train from Mumbai Central, I sent my son to get a taxi. Due to some reasons the taxi came late. Normally a taxi would take one-and-a-half hours from our place to Mumbai Central. We were left with less time than this. I told Behan Pyariji that we might miss the train being morning peak time. She told me: "Deviji (Sharikaji) will take care". To my surprise the taxi reached in less than one hour without stopping at any signal — as soon as we were touching the signal point they were getting green. The taxi driver told me: "Sir, this is the first time I have never stopped at any signal."

Surrendering to Sharikaji would always help. In times of any stress, problem related to anything just close your eyes and see her lotus feet in your heart. It works wonders. I have experienced and realized this on a number of occasions.

She was a great soul rarely born on this earth. Though we always miss her physical presence, still we feel she is around all of us.

Transmitting Spirituality Through Silence

Sudhir Sopory

IN a letter to my father Pt. Jawaharlal Sopory (elder brother of Sharikaji), Swami Īśvara Svarūpa, who was Guru Mahārāj of Devi Sharikaji, wrote:

> Thy respected self do not understand the nowadays situation of blessed Sharika. She should not be advised by thyself in such a way, for her flaming *bhakti* towards Lord of Lords has totally defeated the whole Mayavic Universe.
>
> And in the same letter He added: Such Devīs are rarely found in this world of pains. Her holy existence in your own home will prove the result of thousands of thy good *karma* of the past *janma* if she lives long.

This was written in the year 1928 when Sharikaji, whom we used to address as Didda Pyariji at home, was only fourteen years old.

Sharika Devi was a *yoginī* by birth and as circumstances unfolded, it seemed destined that she would remain a *brahmacāriṇī* and be with her guru and follow the teachings and practices of Trika thought of Kashmir Śaivism and reach the highest and subtlest state of Paramaśiva. Swamiji, Sharika Devi and Prabha Devi lived, studied and practised Śaivism at Ishvar Ashram at Srinagar, Kashmir, where devotees would throng on Sundays to learn from Swamiji and have his and Devi Sharikaji's *darśana*. Since childhood we were blessed with the association of all the three saints, who used to visit our house quite often.

Over the years by the devotion to her guru and through the yogic practices, Sharika Devi elevated herself to the state of Supreme God-consciousness. Her yogic powers have been felt by many who came in contact with her. I am no exception. On other occasions I have written about our interactions with Swamiji and Didda Pyariji.* In this account I want to derive some lessons we can learn on spirituality from the life of Deviji. However, I would like to repeat a couple of personal incidents.

In late 1980s Swamiji had returned from his visit abroad. Deviji along with Prabhaji had come to Jawaharlal Nehru University (JNU) campus where we were staying. It was a small house. The way Sharikaji adjusted without making any demands ever, is something we all need to learn. One day she wanted to have *darśana* of their guru, who was then staying at Mr Kachru's place. Not everyone was allowed there. After Deviji and Prabhaji were escorted inside, I was also allowed on the orders of Swamiji. He put *tilaka* on Deviji and then asked me if I had shown the Lotus Temple to Sharika. I was stunned as only in the morning of the same day I had asked both Sharikaji and Prabhaji if they would like to go to the Lotus Temple. This I told to Swamiji. He immediately got up, asked for his shirt and said "Let us go now and show this temple to Sharika". We all moved and as we were going through the lawns towards the temple, being very hot, Swamiji wanted to take breath and thus stopped. In the scorching sun, Deviji found it very uneasy to see her master sitting. While some other devotees ran to get an umbrella, Deviji unfurled part of her *sāṛī* and kept it over her Master to protect him from the hot rays of the sun. A scene that never gets away

* In the article "The Scientist and the Saint" in *Saṁvidullāsaḥ*, pp. 165-75.

from my memory and that shows the devotion and care she always felt for her Guru Mahārāj.

When Swamiji was to return to Srinagar, He told Deviji that He was going by air and would like her and Prabhaji to accompany him. He also, with a smile on his face, said that the ticket was expensive and if they could not afford it, they should come by train. She did not say anything. Silence was her treasure. When we came back to JNU, in the evening, I offered to buy air tickets for her and Prabhaji. She very reluctantly accepted, on my insistence, however, said, "I will pay this back when I return". The same year she left her mortal body. After some time I got an offer from another institute with higher remuneration and I thought that Deviji has returned not only the fare of the ticket but much more, financially and spiritually. This gift also got further multiplied as Prabha Deviji decided to be with us during winter season and bless us all the time. Being with her constantly reminds us of Swami Īśvara Svarūpa and also Devi Sharikaji as she narrates to us at times her own life at the Ishvar Ashram and the persona of the two great saints.

Over the years I have read some books and heard a few lectures from saints and sages, emphasizing the importance of looking within and observing silence. The stillness and silence actually speaks, they teach us. However, I always wondered, when they themselves write and speak all the time, of course to educate us, how are they going to set an example for others to emulate the practice of silence? Is it at all possible to teach by being calm and still?

I am reminded of a legend written in Osho's book, *The First Principle*. A king once requested Hanyatra, the twenty-fifth successor of Buddha, to come to his court and recite and teach him from the *sūtras* of Buddha. Hanyatra came with an attendant. The king bowed and requested him to start.

However it was the attendant who recited the *sūtras*. The king did not appreciate this and after the recitation was over, he asked Hanyatra, why did not he recite the *sūtras*?

Hanyatra replied: "What! I did not recite, then what else was I doing the whole time?" The king was puzzled and wanted to know the truth. Hanyatra said: "I sat silently, breathing in and breathing out. That was my *sūtra*. What else is there in life? When I breathe in I was aware and when I breathe out I was aware. You should have listened to the rhythm of my breathing. Words are one way to recite and breathing silently is another way to recite." Hanyatra said to the king, "I thought I should give you the real thing".

The story of Hanyatra connects me to the Kashmiri song by Sharikaji. A rough translation of it means: Concentrate on rising and falling breaths, which are like Vasudeva and Devakī, that give birth to Kr̥ṣṇa, the point of concentration between the rising and falling breath that occurs in our body. She compares our body with the prison where Kr̥ṣṇa was born to Vasudeva and Devakī. She practised this and thus remained silently concentrated on the one-pointed superconscious state, the pure Kr̥ṣṇa state of mind that is without fear, desire, attachment but full of purity and truth.

This is what Sharika Deviji was. Teaching the "real" thing through silence, but many of us were not ready to perceive the immense knowledge of Yoga that she wanted to pass on to her disciples; she had mastered the art of communicating without word, without speeches. Swamiji's younger sister told us once, when we visited her daughter's residence in Faridabad, that one day early morning when she went to see Swamiji, she heard a sound resembling that originating from a grinding mill. This sound was emanating from another room. On inquiry, Swamiji told her not to enter that room as Sharika was in her *samādhi* and this is the sound of rising *kuṇḍalinī*, the sound of breath, the sound of silence!

Once Prabhaji told Deviji that she should also engage with some disciples and give discourses, as many other Swamis regularly do. She said, they have been put on that job and let them do so. She did not believe in communicating through long speeches and gaining any limelight and prominence. On the contrary, she would like to live in isolation. Even when she was with her devotees, in reality she was alone, within herself. She had mastered the art of being with, yet being without the persons surrounding her. She would usually communicate through short sentences yet which were loaded with message. Many times these carried dual meaning; one for the common person and another a spiritual message which few could grasp. As Prabhaji narrated to us, once Swamiji told Sharikaji to fetch something from the top shelf and at the same time said that since your height is short you may find difficulty in achieving this. That is why being tall is important, he told her. Came the quick response, "kerosene oil is sold in tall bottles whereas scent is sold in very small bottles".

Her silence and *śakti* within was the flame without smoke. As mortal beings we are tuned to seeing only the smoke. We are used to only learning through verbal communication. In one of her own writings, the last one which Prabha Deviji found after she left her body, she says that though she deliberately lived a silent and subdued life, the scent of her *śakti* was spreading outside; but she managed to escape from glare and pursuit of the public.

Once Prabhaji asked her what will happen to the house when we are away. She said, do you see any house here? I do not. I have my own beautiful house, my body, that is with me and where she always felt the presence of God. She had learnt to empty herself from worldly thoughts and pleasures.

What Swamiji wrote in 1928, that such Devīs are born rarely, this fact we realized very late. We felt that Her presence was consoling, reassuring and divine. But did we learn anything? I only feel bad that even after having such long and close association with Devi Sharikaji, we let ourselves be deprived from imbibing the messages that she was silently communicating to us. As mortals we seek the blessings from such saints for human needs and rarely for spiritual elevation. I pray and bow to her to kindly shower her bliss and *āśirvāda* so that I can get rid of thoughts that burden my mind and give me the source of her energy to concentrate my intellect on the "power within".

Didda Pyariji: The Hidden Saint

Pratibha Bhan

I was very fortunate to have taken birth in the family of "Soporys". I am the youngest child of Pandit Mohan Lalji and Padminiji Sopory. My association with Pūjanīyā Devi Sharikaji commenced the day I was born.

As a child I was unaware of the divine powers of "Didda Pyari", the name given to Deviji by our family, but whenever I looked at her, she looked so serene, spotlessly clean and always smiling.

She was very fond of my father as any elder sister would be. Once we were all eating some fruits, I saw Didda Pyariji pealing the skin of the grapes and then giving it to my father. Noticing this, I enquired from her the reason for this special treatment to him. She was so fond of him that she replied that her brother Bhai Pyareji was too fragile to eat grapes with the skin.

When I was in grade four, she asked me: "Do you know who is in a temple?" I replied "God and who else." To this she smiled and said that your body is also a temple and God is within you. I couldn't understand this deep meaning at that age.

When I was getting married, one day before the wedding, she called me to her room and advised me about the duties and responsibilities of the life ahead. Though a *yoginī*, she had deep insight into the nuances of *gr̥hastha*s.

I would accompany Didda Pyariji to market sometimes for shopping. She would not be tempted by many things on display. I would tell her that things on display were nice and that she could also pick something for her. She would tell me not to get impressed by all display but be choosy as quality matters not the quantity. This advice of her has helped me till today. She was very regal and aristocratic in her style and was not tempted by materialistic things of life. Deviji never lost her temper. She was always cool and contented and had a quick wit.

She talked less yet precise and to the point. Once when Īśvara Svarūpa asked Deviji to fetch something from a shelf which was a little high for her to reach. Because of her inability to reach it, Swamiji commented that Deviji was not tall enough. But on hearing this Deviji promptly replied that "a perfume bottle is always small whereas a kerosene bottle is tall". Īśvara Svarūpa had a great laugh.

Deviji was a great cook. She would make delicious meals. During my summer vacation, sometimes I used to stay in the *āśrama*. Early morning Īśvara Svarūpa, Deviji and Bahen Pyari would go down to the cowshed, feed the Jersey cows and Deviji would milk them. It was a fascinating experience to watch all this. Deviji was a frugal eater but would serve others and make then eat.

Deviji never gave sermons. She was against showing off. Once somebody suggested to her that she would give discourses on various streams of *jñāna* to which she replied politely that she has deputed her workers to do the job. She was so knowledgeable and had attained the highest point in Yoga, yet she was humble and modest. People would be mesmerized in her presence but she would always behave in a casual and simple way. She was miles away from pride and had no ego.

I vividly remember some incidents where her devotees would be patiently waiting for her to finish her tea in *khasoo* and have the remaining tea as a *prasāda,* but Deviji would sense it and would quietly keep the *khasoo* on the floor, so that it became impure to use. There is so much to write about Deviji that I doubt I could do it in my lifetime.

I will never forget the day when Deviji went to her supreme abode. I was lucky to be in Jammu that morning. Didda Pyariji was still and her face was so serene and it looked as if she was in meditation. At one point of time, I felt she was breathing.

So I went closer and checked her pulse. Those thirteen days what Gurudeva did and how he bid farewell to his first *śiṣyā* can never be forgotten.

Didda Pyariji blessed us by being born in the same family. We pray that she continue to shower her blessings on all of us.

My Experiences with Sharikaji

Ashok Dhar

GOD is the dependent friend whose invisible hands work through good angels many a time in the form of humble human beings. One such rare angel has been Sharika Deviji, the idol of innate gentleness and softness.

I would always wonder with awe how simple and submitted to her Master (Swami Lakshman Joo) she was. Her simplicity acted like a shield of her divine persona that put *māyā* in everyone's mind to believe she was one like us. Further, as though this was not enough, we on our foolish part had further enveloped her "aura" by calling her "Didda Pyari" (an elder sister) — she being related to us (she was my father's sister).

There are many incidents that come to my mind when I search the memory of our association with Sharikaji. I would like to share a few of them here.

During February 1979, on the day of my sister's marriage at Jammu, we had invited Sharikaji along with Prabha Deviji to our place. On that day the skies were full of fury. The rain gods were not allowing the cooks to even start the fire for cooking food in the the garden. My mother mentioned this to Deviji who went to the rooftop with an umbrella looking at the entire sky and came down without uttering a single word. The mighty rains stopped after a very short while, much to the relief of everyone.

During my university days it was my annual routine to visit Kashmir in summer vacation and visit "Ishvar Ashram" at Nishat. Sharikaji used to be kind enough to ask me to stay at the *āśrama* and eat there. The divine food eaten by me before Sharikaji is unforgettable. When I used to ask Sharikaji for "naveed" (*prasāda*) she would always tell me to go to Swamiji first. She never put herself before Swamiji.

My mother (Smt. Chanderkanta) tells me that she was told an incident by another of my father's aunts (Mrs Tiku of Allahabad). On one occasion while Mrs Tiku was staying at the old *āśrama* (upper Nishat), she used to stealthily watch Sharikaji waking up in early morning and going out of her room, crossing the wooden berandah. She had seen a lion sitting on the verandah (between the room and bathroom) vacating the pathway for Deviji everyday when she came out.

Sharikaji, accompanied by Prabhaji, graced us with a visit at Hoshiarpur in 1980. They recorded a song for me (which has been written by Sharikaji herself). The song is in subtle and simple Kashmiri and goes like this

sansaar chhui moh janjaal,
vaasna gaal vaasna gaal
vishyan buchhith gasaan chu husyar
vaasna gaal vaasna gaal . . .

Translated simply into English, it would be

This world is a tangle of attachments,
dissolve your desires here
seeing material objects, it (desire) wakes up at slightest excuse;
dissolve your desires here . . .

The song is simple but practising it is quite difficult, as all of us know.

In 1986, while I was posted at Chandigarh, Sharikaji (accompanied by Prabhaji and Mrs Asha Sopory) was kind and gracious enough to visit us for a week. During their visit we went to Haridwar for two days. This visit is always memorable for my family. At Haridwar Sharikaji suggested that we should climb the hill along roadside of "Har ki Pauri". Doing as ordained, I was surprised to see many hermits spending their time in Yoga and worship. I was equally surprised to see how easily Sharikaji traced an old man in his nineties living with little eyesight in a small room on the hill. Hearing almost with his soul's ears, the old man could recognize Sharikaji's voice and felt extreme joy. The Goddess had chosen to give "her *darśana*" to the old man at his doorstep. We had heard during our childhood days that God comes himself to give his *darśana* to a real disciple. Here I was witnessing it myself!

The above accounts are in no way to highlight my family's association with Sharikaji. More importantly it is an attempt to kindle the hope that the great *saṁyāsinī* Sharikaji is still around, guiding us through the journey of life. I bow to Sharikaji in reverence.

The Divine Presence*

Bettina Sharada Bäumer

SHE left quietly and discretely as was her nature. She was spent like a flame, without resistance, going to the abode of Śiva, where she belonged. She has taken bath in a sea of bliss, as she told her Master shortly before leaving — so what else was there to say or do? She said what was to be said, and she had no more to say, because to her everything was clear in that light of the Absolute. Her body had become as light as her mind. Nothing was heavy in her because she was transparent to the Divine Grace.

I cannot forget her last blessing: I knew it was the last. On the day I arrived at Ishvar Ashram, end of January 1991, as if called by her, she was already lying down and I was shocked to see her so weak. I prostrated and she blessed me with such an affectionate caress on my head. When I sat at her feet, she got up and opened her eyes wide. She seemed to pierce me with her look which was both full of love, and full of strength, firm as she was established within. I was not prepared. I could hardly bear her look. Had I been ready, she could have given me *śaktipāta* in that very moment. Her eyes were saying everything, summing up a life at the feet of the Lord, they

* What I wrote spontaneously after receiving the news of Sharika Deviji's *samādhi* in 1991, remains valid and I do not want to dilute it by adding anything. What I have to say about Deviji in a wider context is contained in the introduction to this volume.

were telling that she had reached the heights of *samāveśa*, they were telling that it requires love, gentleness and firmness and a devotion that is undisturbed by any inner or outer shakings. There was a quiet, inner strength in her which, combined with a discrete motherly love, made her a symbol of peace. All that was in her eyes, and a push to have the courage to proceed on this path without a wavering of awareness, devotion and determination. That look was so strong, although her body was almost non-existing, so weak and thin. Her whole soul was in her eyes.

Great saints are often hidden, quiet and discrete. Deviji was a quiet presence near her great Master, effacing herself in His service. Although she had attained self-realization, she assumed a humble role, never showing off her spiritual state or her knowledge. But in her discrete way she was an important adviser to the devotees, mainly female. She helped me immensely in coming nearer to the Master, to act in the right way and in the right moment, to understand his hints and his way of guiding me. Without her I would have despaired many times. She had a motherly eye to tell me when I could go near him, do *praṇāma*, or when I should stay quiet until He would permit me. Only a soul like her who was purified by the constant contact with the Lord could act in this way, guiding inexperienced disciples like me. Sometimes she would intervene like a mediator. He could never refuse her humble but firm request. When I was desperate because the Master had rejected me many times, her one word was reassurance: "He is testing your firmness". If for any reason I did not get *prasāda*, she would make it up by giving me *prasāda*, and I knew it was He who was giving it through her.

A few times it was given to me that I could see her glory. She was then bathed in the same light as her Master, a light which was flowing from within, and flowing all over her body. She then showed me how firmly she was established in her inner nature, *svasvarūpa*, in a quiet, firm clarity. She was beyond the states of emotional devotion, and the contrast between her quiet, humble presence and the mental and physical noise of other devotees was evident. Her very simplicity showed that she was established in the Divine state in any condition — cleaning vegetables, talking to devotees or serving her Master, not to talk of the times of *samāveśa* which she used to hide from others.

Once she told me in a serious mood: People come here for all kinds of purpose and selfish ends, but very few come for God. This was her experience of many years at the feet of the Master. I often felt, it is as if somebody wants to give gold, and the receiver only asks for potatoes. She herself had such gold to give — but who was ready to receive it?

Once I wrote to thank her for her gracious kindness, and she replied through Prabhaji: It is the nature of the river to give freshness and purity to those who come to bathe in it, there is no special merit in the river giving it. This was her natural way of being, and her expressions were equally natural.

At the end she reminded me of my last *darśana* of Mā Anandamayi: in a frail body there was no ego obstructing the Divine presence, whereas our "persons" consist only in obstruction. Once this obstruction is gone, the Divine flows freely through the whole of space.

Now that even the last obstruction is gone, her body itself, there is no end to this flowing of grace. She is more present now than when she was in the body. My only prayer is to be a receiving vessel, empty, receptive and pure.

Three Saintly Women*

Triloki Nath Ganju

THE three saintly women, whose contribution in the rich religio-cultural scene of Kashmir remains unparalleled, appeared at different times in our history: Śaivayoginī Lāl Dêd in the middle age, Alakheśvarī Rūpa Bhavānī towards the end of it and Śaivayogeśvarī Sharikaji in the modern age.

Sharikaji's birth on this earth was the result of her parents' deep, unquestioning devotion to the presiding deity of the Hariparvat hill — the Goddess Śārikā. Both Jiyalal Sopory and Radhika Rani would begin their day with circumambulation of the sacred hill and the mother had always known, during her pregnancy itself, that it was no ordinary being that she was carrying in her womb. Once born, the baby began to show signs of her uniqueness. Even as a toddler, she would prefer to be by herself rather than play like other children. She would be happy to be by herself, wrapped in her silences. Once a doctor visited the family and was taken aback to see the little girl seated in the *padmāsana* pose, lost in meditation, her solemn face glowing with a bright light. It had become her usual practice and in recognition of this, her parents had set apart a room for her, so that she could carry on her meditation undisturbed.

One day the child Sharika suddenly fell unconscious and remained in that state for two whole days. The doctors

* Excerpts from the original Hindi, translated by Neerja Mattoo.

attending on her were puzzled at her condition as there was no obvious indication of any injury. A specialist was called in to examine her, but even he could not diagnose anything — it was just that she seemed to be in a deep, peaceful sleep. After a while he suggested that the whole family collectively sing *bhajanas*, that might wake the child up. Accordingly, the whole family began to sing songs of devotion in one voice and suddenly the child opened her eyes, roused from her sleep, smiling sweetly to the wonder of the family.

As she grew up, she showed a special inclination towards the study of Sanskrit, loving the sonorous *stotras*, so her father arranged for the best scholars of the time to teach her the language and religious scriptures. But even before learning Pāṇini's grammar, she had mastered the language. Gurudeva Swami Lakshman Joo himself used to acknowledge the Devi Sharikaji's flawless Sanskrit scholarship.

Soon, however, a time came when the family began to look for a suitable match for their gifted daughter. In fact, they had found somebody and almost decided on an auspicious date for the engagement, while the subject herself, totally detached from it all, was fully absorbed in Abhinavagupta's deeply philosophical verses. Her rigorous study and constant practice of meditation and Yoga, had firmly set her on a path where she only needed a spiritual mentor now. And she found him in Gurudeva Swami Lakshman Joo, who agreed to teach her all the difficult and subtle concepts of Śaivism. She used to come with her brother for such tutelage and it continued till she had mastered all the texts. During the long time while she studied under him, Gurudeva himself was fully aware of her great powers of equanimity, detachment and concentration. Her devotion to the guru was constant and unswerving, no matter how many uncomfortable situations she had to face, while serving him unflinchingly, and the guru knew it very well. And that is why, when she passed away in

Jammu, he gave instructions that the funeral rites to be held back till he arrived from Srinagar, so that he could perform all the required ceremonies himself, which he did right from the cremation in Jammu to the immersion of her ashes at Haridwar in the sacred Gaṅgā.

Mother Sharika

Pramod Sharma

I USED to visit Ishvar Ashram, Nishat, Srinagar, on almost every Sunday during 1988 to March 1990 to have a *darśana* of Swami Lakshman Joo. During those visits, the Ishvar Ashram appeared to me as a most beautiful divine world which like a magnet pulled me for my Sunday visits to watch the divine play of Swamiji in the *āśrama*. The Ishvar Ashram was known for its divine light, Swami Lakshman Joo, a great authority on Kashmir Śaivism. Swamiji was the greatest saint I had met, seen, heard or read about. Besides Swamiji, two Devīs were also residing in Ishvar Ashram but I had yet to be introduced to them. Only after some time did I come to know that the kind lady who was guiding my spiritual journey on the instruction of Swamiji by sharing books on Kashmir Śaivism was actually one of the two Devīs. Her name is Prabha Devi, whom, later, I started revering as my spiritual Master.

On one Sunday, when I was standing outside the veranda of the *āśrama*, a place where I used to interact with Prabha Deviji, I met the other Deviji standing in the veranda. I wished her by offering my humble *praṇāma* with folded hands and she said, "It is extremely good that you have become fond of the spiritual path in this young age". Casually, I replied that it was because of her grace. Deviji spoke in very soft manner and corrected my reply, "No, *śaktipāta* has been bestowed upon you". I noticed that I had casually mentioned that it is her grace but she spoke very authoritatively that it was *śaktipāta*.

The word *śaktipāta'* was new to me and I did not really understand then, as to what she meant. Though Devi Sharikaji was about seventy-five year old then, she appeared much younger and a very peaceful soul. She had the innocence of a young child but a deep mystical maturity behind the eyes as if she belonged to another world. Because of her simplicity and naturalness, any human being would be at peace in her presence. During those Sunday visits, I often used to have *darśana* of Devi Sharikaji attending to Swamiji and obediently following his instructions. Once or twice I saw Swamiji getting annoyed and speaking to her harshly in Kashmiri language which I did not understand. I never saw her speaking to anyone. I recall her as walking in the garden near Swamiji, self-absorbed and with bowed head.

I left Kashmir in March 1990 due to acts of terrorism in Kashmir Valley. I lost contact with Swamiji and Ishvar Ashram, as I moved around to various parts of the country in connection with my profession. However, I could never forget Swami Lakshman Joo and Ishvar Ashram and always felt that I was missing something within me. The Kashmiri migrants were scattered and spread all over the country and I could not locate the whereabouts of Swamiji till I heard the news of his departing from this world on national TV. The news gave me a great shock as Swamiji was always in my heart and his photo in my home temple. Needless to say that it came as a great spiritual relief when I could contact again Prabha Deviji in May 1993 at Jammu/Srinagar and started a desperate cycle of correspondance with her. I am extremely grateful to Susri Prabha Deviji for her selfless guidance in making me understand my own self as well as Kashmir Śaivism. She gave me the greatest spiritual relief and guidance. Through Prabha Deviji, I came to know that Susri Sharika Deviji has departed from this mortal world on 2 February 1991 at Jammu in the house of Shri Moti Lal Sopory. She had fallen seriously ill in

January 1991 and Shri Moti Lal Sopory and his sister Smt. Sarojini Ganju brought her to Jammu on 29 January 1991. A few months later the revered Master of Susri Sharika Devi, Swami Lakshman Joo also departed from this mortal world on 27 September 1991, as if to join her in the world of Lord Śiva.

This is all I knew about Sharika Devi. But as if this was not enough, she started slowly revealing herself to me after her death. The other part of this write-up is what she has revealed to me after her death in silence.

Sharika Devi was the chief disciple of Swami Lakshman Joo. She manifested in physical body for seventy-eight years in Kashmir Valley during 1913 to 2 February 1991. She was born in a very educated and prosperous Kashmiri Pandit family in Srinagar. Her father Shri Jiya Lal Sopory was the first qualified civil engineer of Kashmir and mother Smt. Radhika Rani was a very pious and religious woman. The Sopory family had six children, three daughters and three sons, and she was the fourth child. The Soporys initially lived at Sarafkadal and later shifted to Wazir Bagh area of Srinagar. The culture of the Sopory family was more modern and advanced as compared to other local Kashmiri Pandits of Srinagar, during those days. This was due to the reason that head of family Shri Jiya Lal Sopory had migrated to Srinagar from Lucknow in 1903 at the age of twenty-three years. Shri Jiya Lal had been brought up and educated at Lucknow and Lahore and later received the civil engineering education from the premier engineering college of India at Roorkee. During those days, there were not many people in India with his academic background.

Shri Satchitanandaji a senior disciple of Mahatma Mangat Ramji of Santa Ashram, Jagadhari, visited Ishvar Ashram for three/four months in 1957 and kept on coming back to *āśrama* for a number of years. With the grace of Swami Lakshman

Joo, Goddess Sarasvatī manifested in his heart and he wrote Sharika Baudh[1] which says:

> When Sharikaji was twelve years old, supreme dispassion came in her heart. She was infatuated with love for God and therefore fire of separation with God flared up. She neglected attention to her food and clothing. She was agitated and was unable to restore harmony of heart and she had hope only of her lover (i.e. God). When she was thirteen years old, with the grace of God she met her guru who was a great saint and at the feet of Īśvara Svarūpa Lakshman Joo, she immersed herself wholeheartedly. She acquired means and found salvation as her guru Īśvara Svarūpa blessed her. All her delusions and wandering vanished and her life became full of peace and grace. All her worldly and religious obligations were fulfilled. Cycle of births and deaths was destroyed and Sharika became immortal. The greatest guru Lakshman Joo is a supreme spirit and Śiva Svarūpa and with his compassionate graceful glance on Sharika, she achieved an incomparable, purest and unadulterated state of self.

Susri Prabha Deviji who spent her full life with her writes in the book *Bhāvārcana*:

> At her birth, she was a very healthy and beautiful baby and because of her divine physique she was named "Sharika Devi".

In very early childhood also she used to get up at 4 a.m. in the morning and sit in meditation posture for an hour, morning as well as evening. Swami Lakshman Joo gave her experience of *samādhi* (self-enlightenment) at a very young age (before she was nineteen years old) at Gopī-Tīrtha through *śaktipāta* in presence of her brother Mohan Lal. She was endowed with the nature of self-relating spontaneously.

---

1 *Sharika Baudh*, published by Ishvar Ashram in Hindi.

Several virtues were visible in her person such as simplicity, modesty, egolessness, inner stability, respecting herself, continuous engagement in her spiritual practice and fearlessness. Each act of her manifested sole devotion toward Gurudeva, affection, devotion to duty, firm faith, abundance of genuine devotion toward God. In spite of being fearless, she was always scared of Gurudeva. She was affectionately inclined toward her guru, brothers and sisters. On noticing any disciple being perplexed by Gurudeva, the tender heart of Deviji used to become compassionate and like a mother she used to console them, get him *prasādam,* etc. from Guru Mahārāj and make them happy. On one side she was serious in her nature; there was childlike simplicity on the other side. Infusion of sense of humour was also observed in her speech now and then. Whenever a little anger of Gurudeva, hurt the tender lotus heart of Deviji for a few moments, she would write poetry in Kashmiri to refresh her lotus-like mind. Her poetry was mostly based on her spiritual practice. She would recite this poetry in low melodious pitch. I was always awaiting this and would write down her poem. In this manner a few of her poems are saved. She was ever alert and devoted to her spiritual practice. She would get up at 3 a.m. in the night and sit on her *āsana* and instantly get absorbed in meditation. After taking bath, etc. in the morning, she would get engaged in service of her guru at 6 a.m. Having spent her whole life in the *āśrama,* she was not attached with any materialistic thing or any person. She would not check the time to sit in meditation practice. She used to say, will a thirsty person check time to drink water? Similarly for the thirst of union with God, it is useless to wait for appropriate time. This thirst can only be satisfied by constant practice day and night. In spite of being always absorbed in awareness of the Supreme, she never used to reveal this. She was always keeping her head in bowed posture, following respectfully the command of guru.

Whenever she invoked God, she felt delighted calling God as "Infinite" and "store house of beauty". Having spent her whole life under the refuge of Gurudeva, she was a liberated person in life in true sense. Having surrendered her individuality at the feet of Gurudeva, she became immortal forever.

From early childhood Sharikaji had interest in meditation, praying to God and reading religious scriptures. With such nature, interests and lifestyle she came in contact with Swami Lakshman Joo. In 1932, she took formal initiation from him at the age of ninteen years. Swamiji gave her initiation in *rāja-yoga*. As per *Haṭha-yoga Pradīpikā, rāja-yoga, samādhi, unmanī, manonmanī, amaratva, laya, tattva, śūnyāśūnya, paramapada, amanaska, advaita, nirālamba, nirañjana, jīvanmukti, sahaja* and *turīya* — all these words announce the same Reality. In 1934, when she was twenty-one years old, her father constructed a house for her adjoining Swamiji's Ashram on Ishber Mountain. She lived there for twenty-eight years doing her spiritual practices under the guidance of her Gurudeva, Swami Lakshman Joo. In 1962, she moved into the present Ishvar Ashram at Ishber village. She lived here for another twenty-nine years before departing from this mortal world. Thus she spent fifty-seven years in the *āśrama* serving God and her Master Swami Lakshman Joo, day and night. We rarely find many saints in this world who have served their Master for so long and that too wholeheartedly and with true devotion. Swami Lakshman Joo also paid befitting tributes to her on the occasion of her demise. The great guru personally supervised and performed all the rituals as per scriptures and also danced like Lord Śiva at the time of her death. Swamiji also referred her as incarnation of Parā-Śakti and created a *mantra* on her — *para bhairavelīnyai parāśaktyai śrī śārikā devyai namo namaḥ'*, on the occasion of her leaving the physical body.

One of Sharika's poems is quoted below:

Vāsanā[2]

This world is a snare of delusion and attachments
Root out the impressions of objectivity from memory
Black Time snake has spread its large hood's doors
Root out the impressions of objectivity from memory.

The flame of ignorance is increasing its luminosity
Passion, etc. (i.e. passion, wrath and greed) became the fuel
The Indwelling Being becomes helpless, pitiable and poor
Obtains fruits and performs deeds.
Root out the objective impressions from memory.

Unconscious objective impressions in memory are like a sleeping cobra
Spiritless mind is ever sick
By repeatedly remembering the taste of objects
Becomes fully alert to indulge
Root out objective impressions from memory.

Retreat from objective world
Recognize your own Śiva existence
Contemplate only on this mantra
The whole world is my existence
Realize Śiva existence on first impression
Root out objective impressions from memory.

This only is called burning ground
This only is Śiva's place of abode
Idol of duality becomes ashes

---

[2] Sri Sharikaji's poetry "Vāsanā" appeared in *Malini* magazine of September 1996. The poetry was translated by Makhan Lal Kukiloo from Kashmiri to Hindi. The writer has translated the poem from Hindi to English with the help of Swami Yoganand of Brahmarishi Bawraji Ashram, Virat Nagar, Pinjore. The writer expresses gratitude to Swami Yoganand.

Recognize old existence after burning memories
Root out objective impressions from memory.

States of deception, cheating, attachment exist no more
The empirical being understands on awakening
Remain ever absorbed crossing over time will easily come
Root out objective impressions from memory.

I thank Mother Sharikaji for revealing herself to me in her silence.

Śaktisvarūpā Sharika Devi

Yogendra Tiku

I AM blessed that I have been asked to write and express my feelings towards my guru, Svayaṁ Śaktisvarūpā Sharika Deviji. I can't count my blessings enough that my guru has showered upon me, and continues to do so. I am a simple, ignorant, mortal, human being. It is due to some good *karma*s of my various past lives that my guru Sharika Deviji blessed me with her love and guidance. Saints like her take birth in this mortal world to guide ignorant people like me, and make them sail through this world like a lotus leaf. I am extremely fortunate that I opened my physical eyes in this world, connected with the family of Deviji. Therefore, since my early childhood, I have been meeting Deviji and *parama pūjanīya* Śrī Īśvara Svarūpa. My early memories of Ishvar Ashram (Srinagar) are that my family and other family members used to visit *āśrama* to meet Swamiji and Devi Sharikaji, whenever we visited Srinagar. There we were taken care of by Devi Sharikaji and Devi Prabhaji. I used to feel at home at the *āśrama*. We used to have lunch or tea, as the time schedule would permit, and then have *prasāda* and leave. I particularly used to sit mostly with Deviji. Here I would also like to mention that my grandmother was one of the earliest disciples of Swami Īśvara Svarūpa. She would always ask us to behave in certain manner in front of Swamiji. I was at that age somehow scared of Swamiji. May be as a child I would find him a little serious and a towering personality.

I am told by my parents that the year I was born, Swami Īśvara Svarūpa had come to our home in Allahabad, since that was the year of Mahākumbha at Prayāg. So I take this opportunity to believe that Lord Śiva had come personally to bless me, after I was born. This thought always stirs my being and warms my existence. After that year, Swamiji, Devi Sharikaji and Devi Prabhaji visited us a few more times in Allahabad. They would stay at our home only. I remember, one of their visits coincided with Mahāśivarātri festival. That year our Śivarātri *pūjā* was presided over and performed by Swamiji himself.

We children used to play with Swamiji, and in the evenings, all the family members would sit together and perform *sandhyā* (prayers). I remember learning and reading *Stuti Candrikā* at that time, when I was barely seven or eight years old.

I am talking about all this, simply to emphasize how close we were with Deviji and Swamiji. At that age I always used to consider Devi Sharikaji as my aunt only. I was a child and could never understand her greatness, in not even trying to show an iota of her Śakti.

Deviji remained like that throughout her life. Never, even for a moment, showing that she was a *jīvanmuktā*, a realized soul and an incarnation of Śakti on this earth. She would always talk less and let others hog the limelight. The reason being she herself was always immersed in the light of consciousness (*cetanā*), therefore these lesser attractions were of no meaning to her. That is the greatness of the evolved saints, that they keep hiding their real state and their true identity, and act like normal human beings in the presence of ordinary people like me.

Deviji always set an example, in front of us, that how a true disciple should behave in front of his or her master. I clearly remember, ladies in the *āśrama* coming and asking her for blessings, but she would always direct them towards Swamiji and tell them, why do you come to me, when incarnated Lord Śiva, himself is sitting there, in front of you. But her silent blessings were always bestowed upon the needy.

She would very subtly sometimes point out or say something, about the forthcoming events, which we could understand only after those events had come true. I personally have experienced many such things. There was a time, when I had just come back to India from Nairobi and wanted to settle in Bombay (Mumbai). I told her about my wish. She very lightly, in her gentle voice, asked me, "why do you want to go to Bombay, why don't you settle in Delhi?" This was in 1989. My family was at Allahabad at that time. My interest was in performing arts, hence I wanted to settle in Bombay. So I started thinking what will I do in Delhi, when my family is in Allahabad, and I want to go to Bombay to pursuit my career in acting, etc. I carried on with my set plan of action and moved to Bombay. As destiny would have it, I stayed in Bombay just for a few months and didn't like the lifestyle and pace of the city. Gradually things started taking shape and all the pieces of jigsaw puzzle fitted into its places and I finally had to settle in Delhi.

Devi Sharikaji was very selective in choosing her disciples and had given *dīkṣā* only to a few ladies. I somehow, always wanted to be blessed by her grace and wanted *dīkṣā* from her only. Once I was sitting in the Ishvar Ashram, and like a child asks a toy from her mother, asked her to bless me with *dīkṣā*. She immediately asked for a *jantrī* (yearly astrological compilations) and gave me a date. I just couldn't believe my luck. On the said date, I was blessed with her grace. I am extremely proud that I am the only male *śiṣya* (disciple) of Devi Sharikaji. She remains to me my omnipotent mother and guru.

Though Deviji is now referred to as "Para Bhairava Līnī", but she is present here with all grace among us, all the time. She is Bhairava Śakti and present in even the tiniest atom of all the worlds. I have never felt her absence. I fail in describing her glory and grace. I know, one has to just close eyes and ask for her grace, and there she fills our complete existence, with her grace and blessings. In the form of all-pervading Śakti, she is taking care of this world and her devotees all the time.

Guru! Please ignore our shortcomings and keep guiding us and showering upon us your blessings for ever.

An Embodiment of Śakti

H.N. Jalali

In 1958 I came in contact with Sharikaji at Ishwar Ashram and the association continued till her *nirvāṇa* in 1991. During my visits I would keenly observe her way of *sādhanā*. She was completely different from her guru. As per the desire of her guru she used to serve him outwardly but inwardly she had adopted the *mantra* of silence for her spiritual attainment. Whenever I used to see her she would be in the mood of *abhyāsa*. While doing daily chores in serving her master she never transgressed her limit of *lakṣmaṇa-rekhā* set for her by her guru. Never I saw her losing temper and she always received people with a smile. Whenever somebody asked for her blessing, she would say "God will help you". These four words from her lips would mesmerize the seeker who would feel the help of God. She had a vision and would tell the wrong doer in a lovable voice that henceforth the wrong should not be repeated. Briefly I would like to mention some of her supernatural powers.

Once, I had gone to see R.N. Kikloo, a great realized soul in his own way, and enquired from him about the spiritual status and realization of Sharikaji. He said, she is Śārikā Mātā incarnate. On my insistence to elaborate it Kikloo narrated that once he had gone to meet Swamiji in the *aśrama*. He was sitting on the veranda, Sharikaji too was there a little away from Swamiji. A thought flashed in his mind: Is there any relationship between the two beyond the relationship of a guru and a disciple? Immediately he turned his mind off from the thought, offered *praṇāma* to Swamiji and left for home. After taking lunch he slept and saw a dream in which Sharika Devi appeared as Mā Śārikā with eighteen arms. He woke up, was shaken. Early next day, he went to the *āśrama* and bowed before Sharikaji and Swamiji. Sharikaji looked at him and smiled. He was convinced that Sharikaji is Mā incarnate.

She had *trikāla dṛṣṭi*. Once Swamiji was giving discourse under the *chinār* trees and I too was present. Swamiji said the features of the guru should be that he or she should have no deformity, no disability, no ignorance, etc. I interrupted and pointed out to Swamiji that our guru is perfect and why he is telling us all this. He banged me and tears trickled from my eyes and I left the place with a heavy heart towards the *āśrama*. To my surprise Sharikaji appeared before me and said, "don't worry, you have been blessed by gurujī". I was surprised how she came to know about it. I am convinced that she had *trikāla dṛṣṭi*.

There are many instances in my life when she knew what was in my mind and would respond in a subtle way. Once she was sitting in a chair facing Hari Parbat and I asked her what types of clothes Devī is wearing. Promptly she said "white". Sharikaji was always wearing a white *sāṛī* and her answer made me to understand that Mā is sitting before me. Once her younger sister Prabha Devi who was staying with her in the *āśrama* asked her how it is that people approach you many a time for getting their work done. She said, they know who will take their application to Lord Śiva like a postman. Swamiji had great reverence and affection for Sharikaji. Many a time he would direct the devotess to take *prasāda* from Sharikaji and this would give great satisfaction to the devotees.

I am married to Santosh Kaul (Talib), the daughter of her elder sister. To my knowledge Sharikaji never asked her guru for any special blessing for us. That would be against the norms of the *āśrama*. She had no prejudice, no hate, no favouritism and never believed in caste or creed since all were equal to her. For attaining spiritual awareness from her guru she had to cross a lot of hurdles and obstructions and had to undergo severe tests with success, otherwise she could have not lived in the *āśhrama* her entire life.

In the end I would like to say Sharikaji will remain a legend in the history of Ishwar Ashram of Ishber for all times to come. Whosoever wants spiritual blessing must have forbearance, stamina, discipline and high integrity like Sharikaji and Swamiji.

Sharikaji was an embodiment of Śakti and purity, may her blessing continue to shower on all of us. Swamiji and Sharikaji came to this world to bestow blessing and love to all their devotees like Lord Śiva and Mā Śārikā.

Homage to Sharika Mā

Manmohan Dhar

Sharika Mā was one from above,
An ocean of peace and infinite love.

Behind her calm face was yoginī's fire,
That none could dare nor come near.

Her motherly smile, on her Divine face,
Had the power of Kālī and Durgā's grace.

She lived in this world as witness Supreme,
Untouched by grief of life's evanescent dream.

She has gone from where she came,
To her Lord's abode, after finishing her game.

Devī Mā

Jaya Kaul

I WISH I could describe the face which is a mixture of compassion and innocence like Mīrā clad in white, with a childlike smile on face, soft spoken, full of compassion, words fall like petals of rose and fill the mind with fragrance, rendering a soothing touch to the wounds invisible.

Mā! I have placed you at the altar of my mind. I close my eyes and see you seated there. Mā, I shall worship you in my own *mandira*. Never should the world know that you are there.

Mā, the world is so cruel; it will snatch you away from me,
I have lost all my prized possessions; in fact I had to surrender all my love; I don't want to lose you too,
Oh! no, I won't let anyone see, where I have kept you.
I won't ask you to give one your love
It comes to me without asking.
I pray to you Mā, give some strength
so that I don't recede into nothingness
There is vastness of seas behind your two small eyes,
while gazing at them, one loses oneself completely
with one dip the soul gets purified, pettiness of self is lost, we become just one
An idol of marble, shedding peace and love
Thick black hair, uncared for
Running over your shoulders,
fills "Gaṅgā Mā"

Śiva held "Gaṅgā Mā" in His jaṭā *but Śakti lets it flow to her children*
How can a Mother hold anything back from her children?
Mā, make us worthy of sharing your blessing without discrimination.
Mā! keep this unworthy child, somewhere near you
For I need you most.

Salutations[1]

Gaurishori

The Śakti incarnate of the Kashmiri world
Our salutations to her, again and again!
Sharika the goddess of this abode of saints
Chose to be born to the saintly Rādhikā Rānī,
In the bright fortnight of Maghar *in 1913,*
To bless and bestow glory on the Sopory family.
In Jia Lal Sopory's rich household, an ascetic daughter,
Secluding herself, chose a celibate life.
Though resident in her father's mansion,
Devoted entirely to serving the guru,
Not for her the joys and comforts of night and day.
Dignified and softly solemn, deeper than the deepest,
A secret yoginī, *never revealed to the crowds!*
Discreet and dutiful, ever obedient to the guru,
A perfect saint, endowed with powers, yet high in compassion
The keystone of a guru-śiṣya *edifice,*
The shining spirit of the Ishvar Ashram!
Sharp intellect, subtle and untainted mind of a saṁnyāsī,
Ever-absorbed in meditation, an ascetic supreme,
All her breaths dedicated to serve her guru!
Like a mother feeding her child, her Gurudeva.
Preparing and distributing food like the cornucopia she was,
Lovingly tending the vessels used by her guru,

[1] Translated from Kashmiri by Neerja Mattoo.

While still making each guest feel at home.
Such wisdom, firmly based on true faith!
Never indulged in a luxurious bed,
She stayed awake through the night,
Intent, lest she miss the sound of her Guru's footstep.
A sandal tree bestowing cool shade to all,
Spinning the finest yarn of the so'ham *chant with her breath.*
An untouched celibate and ascetic,
Yet showing to householders the right path
Of true knowledge,
Meditation and the equitable way.
Ever a support to the poor and the helpless,
Finding a resolution to all their dilemmas.
A treasure house of love and motherly concern,
A veritable Lāl and Rūpa Dêd,
Ever-focused on the Absolute.
Engaged in daily chores, yet fully absorbed in meditation.
The twin angels of the Sopory family,
Descended to live on this abode of saints —
Sharika and Prabha, the chosen messengers of Divinity!
Let all pay heed and listen,
To these chief disciples of Īśvar Svarūpa!
Resplendent in glory, she outstripped the guru,
Who constantly chanted, "Sharika Sharika"
In the dark fortnight of Phāgun, she flew into eternity
And now we celebrate her centenary
When the moon and the stars join us in joy!
With folded hands Gaurī makes this offering of words.

III
Glimpses of Deviji's Wit and Wisdom

15 October 1978

It was on a Monday that Īśvara Svarūpa had gone up to God's House to observe his vow of silence. When he came down, he realized that the key to the lower house had been left behind. Instead of going back all the way, he decided to spend the night in the veranda. Meanwhile Kamalaji brought her full bunch of keys. Deviji and she tried each of the keys, but none worked. Then Prabha picked up a key and chanting aloud, "Jai Gurudeva", inserted it into the lock and it opened at once. The next day, Deviji, commenting on this, said to Īśvara Svarūpa: "When a mere lock refuses to respond to a strange key, how is it that married women today are ready to be intimate with other men?"

3 January 1979

Īśvara Svarūpa and Santramji were in conversation with each other, discussing when the restlessness of an individual mind could find complete stillness and be finally at peace. Deviji could not stop herself and intervened: "Sir, how can these creepers of desire die when everyone, instead of letting them parch, is busy watering them? Not a leaf is allowed to wither away. As a result, they thrive, lusciously green. One should never have allowed them to take root in the first instance. Caring about them is like nourishing them." Īśvara Svarūpa and Santramji could only say that what she said was really true.

5 January 1979

Īśvara Svarūpa had got the curtains of his room washed. A couple of them were quite worn out. Īśvara Svarūpa asked Deviji to iron them very carefully so that they do not tear further. Deviji answered with a very serious expression: "These curtains cannot even cover their own selves properly, how can they curtain others? We should fear such curtains and such people, who can neither shield themselves nor those whom they are supposed to shield."

7 January 1979

It was eight in the evening. The heavy traffic of people all through the day had made Deviji quite fed up. When all the disciples had finally left, Īśvara Svarūpa asked her to lock up all the doors and sit in silent meditation. Deviji responded softly: "One locks up to keep one's possessions safe. People have come and gone, but the impression of their character traits is stamped on our minds, so what is the point of locking up now? A thief at night can only steal things, but the burden of what the people have left here with us — what about that? So why lock up now?" Īśvara Svarūpa responded: "Do what you think best."

13 January 1979

We were on our way to Allahabad. We spent a comfortable night in the train compartment. As soon as it was morning and we had finished our daily rituals, Deviji turned her attention to herself, combing her hair, arranging her *sari*, patting her face with her hands. A lady sitting near us was watching all her actions. Noticing this, Deviji turned to her and said: "What are you looking at? It is morning and every *pujārī* is busy with cleaning up his temple. Aren't we all the priests of our own body-temple? That is why we too begin the day with tidying it up and trying to make it look presentable. This body is a temple in which God resides, hence it is our prime duty to keep it clean."

10 February 1979

It was 7 o'clock on Monday morning. After his vow of silence, Īśvara Svarūpa was seated in the veranda, to have his tea. I told Deviji that having had yoghurt with my dinner last night, I had fallen into deep sleep and could not wake up in time and, as a result, I was feeling uneasy. Īśvara Svarūpa was quietly listening, when Deviji suddenly said, "I prefer deep sleep rather than this wakefulness in which there is no concentration on one fixed point, no single-mindedness, except for the daily routine. It is that state, in my opinion, which should be considered sleep. So why regret not having woken up? Now that you are awake, keep your mind fixed on the One throughout the whole day and then waking up late will have no meaning. Wake up now, keep practising and stay truly awake — that is the way to find God. There are so many who tell their prayer beads mechanically, while their minds are going in circles like the wheels of a watermill! What is the worth of such 'meditation'?"

11 March 1979

While translating Abhinavagupta's *Gītā* into Hindi, I was looking for the word *bhrama* (illusion) in the dictionary. Deviji was sitting next to me and commented in her simple, gentle way: "Do you notice that 'Brahmā', who is the life of everything, is spelt with a simple "b" and *bhrama*, which means illusion, has given itself the added weight of an 'h' with the 'b'. Actually, great people always assume a modest demeanour, while the shallow ones give themselves such airs!" These words roused everyone's attention.

14 March 1979

It was 9 o'clock in the morning when a couple of women came into study room. Deviji asked them how much time they spent in prayer. One of them replied: "Mahārāj, what can we say? Our household chores leave us hardly any time and before we know it, it is night." Deviji responded: "Household chores will not be over even till death. I suggest that you give yourself a pause whenever possible and fix your mind on God. Analysing deep truths will keep your mind free from restlessness even while you are attending to your mundane chores. The idea is that you do all your normal daily activities, but without getting possessed by them. That is how you can keep your mind pure".

16 March 1979

Some visiting ladies were discussing how householders should treat one another, everyone expressing her views. One of them said: "What should we do when the relatives around us treat us badly? Then we have to treat them the same way." Deviji simply said: "You should keep your broom of right behaviour so that no filth has a chance to gather. That is how your heart and mind will stay clean. The purity of your heart will surely influence all those who are against you and they will automatically begin to love you."

20 March 1979

It was evening. There was a power breakdown and Īśvara Svarūpa was trying to light a gas lamp. He had set a match to the mantle, but it was not igniting properly. As a result, the mantle could not burn properly and shed expected light. Watching this, Deviji said softly: "As long as a person is not consumed in the fire of penance, the light of true illumination will not appear. Light comes only after the burning. The mantle must burn fully to emit light. Hence one must be ready to sacrifice, to do penance, in order to become enlightened." Gurudeva Īśvara Svarūpa agreed and said to me: "Remember the profound thought that has been communicated."

22 March 1979

Several women, totally devoid of any spiritually, had come and established themselves in the *āśrama*. Deviji found their presence very disturbing, but Īśvara Svarūpa would defend them and even scold Deviji in this regard. One day he was sitting in the garden when a bevy of *mynahs* flew down and began to hop around. Watching them, Īśvara Svarūpa said: "I don't know why I dislike these strutting *mynahs*." Taking advantage of the opportunity, Deviji gently remarked: "Because there is no grace in their walk and they eat even filth and still strut proudly with their heads held high. That is why we too don't like those who, far from having any realization of their shortcomings, carry themselves around proudly, as though they were the epitome of perfection."

25 March 1979

Deviji was seated in the veranda when I noticed that her *sari* had a couple of holes in it. When I asked her why she was wearing a torn *sari*, she looked at me intently, saying: "The holes in the *sari* are visible to you, but what about the holes in the body? How come you never noticed them? These externals should not concern you, try to keep your sight always turned inwards." This gentle admonishment silenced me.

27 March 1979

Our helper Gopinath was smoking secretly, when we called out for him. He came quickly, his nostrils still emitting smoke. Deviji asked him, with a serious face: "When did you light the cooking range? One can see smoke rising from the two burners." Grinning with embarrassment at this gentle reprimand, he slunk out.

22 April 1979

Īśvara Svarūpa's birthday was to be celebrated on 23 April. All of us, his disciples, were sitting around him on the veranda. It was night and winged insects — perhaps ants with wings — were swarming around the lamp. One devotee asked:

"Where have these butterflies come from?" Deviji replied: "Perhaps these are silkworms who have acquired wings." At this another one said: "It is not the season for silkworms. They only appear in June and July." Deviji, after a moment's reflection spoke: "You are right. Here in the *āśrama*, we are as though in a boat, unaware in which flow of time it is sailing on the waters of this world. We do not even realize the passage of months or which month it is, so engrossed are we. If it goes on like this, we will not even be aware of our death, rather welcome it with joy and depart from this world for ever."

15 May 1979

Deviji was growing weaker physically and she took ill. Some devotees came to enquire about her health. Deviji spoke to them sweetly: "In the spiritual sense there is nothing wrong with me. This physical illness cannot afflict my consciousness. I am happy in my mind, so my illness will also disappear."

20 May 1979

Deviji was asked by one woman devotee how one should worship God. Deviji answered with an example: "Just as a cow, tempted by the green grass at a distance, is pulled back by her keeper tugging at the tether, so that she stays on the path and goes forward, a human being too is pulled away from material pursuits by God-consciousness and attracted towards spiritual practice. This is what is known as *śaktipāta*. Meditating upon the Eternal in a constant state of practice is like the rope that guides one to the desired destination. That is known as God's grace."

20 June 1979

It was a Monday when Deviji and several devotees including me were conversing about spiritual matters. We talked about the practice of meditation, with almost everyone complaining of the restlessness of the mind and consequent difficulty in concentration. Deviji quite simply said: "While meditating, think of this mind as a clock, with your inhalation as its one needle and exhalation as the other. Keep these two needles in one straight line, one on 12 and the other on 6, then fix your mind on them. That is how you will be able to fix your mind on one point and concentrate while meditating."

27 June 1979

Īśvara Svarūpa, Deviji and myself were sitting in the veranda, when I asked him: "You treat the two of us as if we are of no consequence, while the other devotees are allowed to do what they please, you never say anything to them." Deviji intervened: "What do you mean by being treated as of no consequence? One's boat should be the one which has no hole in it, so that it can reach the destination safely without anybody's help and without any fear of sinking. It should not be the one that requires frequent repairs. If your boat is sound, fixedness of mind is the only boatman you need who can row it to the destination." Listening to this, Īśvara Svarūpa said: "She has communicated the truth to you, remember it always."

30 June 1979

It was evening. We were sitting in the veranda with Santramji, talking about our experiences of the body becoming weaker day-by-day, when Deviji intervened with a gentle, yet grave voice: "In this world, a human being's life becomes useless after the age of fifty. A joyous welcome greets one at birth, but as one advances towards old age, a sense of weariness sets in, just as what happens in the case of a pilgrim, who is exhausted during his difficult trek and wishes that he could reach his destination. We too are exhausted by our journeys of multiple births and deaths and long to reach our final destination and find eternal rest. But that goal is never found and our tiredness finds no relief." This put everyone into a thoughtful mood.

5 July 1979

One day a newly-wed couple came and stood before Īśvara Svarūpa while we were all in the veranda. He asked me who they were. I looked at the girl's face and said: "Sir, she is the daughter of your sister's son." Her husband was from Kerala and quite dark, while she was very fair. After they left, Deviji said: "I had never seen night and day together, today I was privileged to see both at the same time, in the same place." Īśvara Svarūpa added: "*Pūrṇimā* (night of the full moon) and *amāvasyā* (night of the new moon) appeared before me simultaneously, joined together!"

10 July 1979

Deviji, Dinanathji and myself were sitting in the veranda, when the subject of court cases came up. Dinanathji said: "When a landlord wants the tenant to vacate his house, the tenant goes to the court, asserting that he won't do so." I said that such things happen because of the selfish nature of human beings, and that after all, the house belongs to the owner, so why should there be litigation. After listening to us, Deviji commented: "Aren't all of us too tenants who inhabit this body-house? The owner of this property, God, leases it out to us, and then sends notices from time to time: A notice when old age approaches, a notice when teeth fall out and so on. Not realizing the import of these notices, we go to the lawyer/doctor, who gives temporary relief through his legal/medical skill, but a time comes when our suit is sure to be dismissed. Then comes Death, to execute our eviction. Are we not occupying this body thinking of it as our permanent home?"

13 July 1979

Īśvara Svarūpa, Deviji and I were sitting in the veranda as usual, when we began to talk about the large number of foreigners coming to the *āśrama*. Īśvara Svarūpa said that if we wished, they would come in even larger numbers. In her gentle way, Deviji remarked: "Maharaj, I have come to the conclusion that one should assume the form of a small, light boat which has no burden even of a roof. One must have only superficial relationships with others, forging an inner relationship with no one else but God, that is how our boat will sail easily towards its distination. The worst storm can then do no harm to it." Īśvara Svarūpa heard her through and became thoughtful for some time.

30 July 1979

Deviji, Dinanathji and I were talking about *pañcakṛtya*s. Deviji elaborated thus: "The *yogī* who practises *pañcakṛtya*s has no time to get trapped into delusions created by emotions like anger. He is totally absorbed in the joy of his practice and lost in his effort to handle the *sudarśana cakra*! In fact, Lord Kṛṣṇa's *sudarśana cakra* is nothing but this very practice of *pañcakṛtya*. The *yogī*s who have not yet overcome anger are like a boatman who rows his boat very fast for some time and then rests his oars and lets the boat drift on its own. In the same way these *yogi*s too give up their yogic practice, but do not give up anger. They have not yet reached the stage of *pañcakṛtya*."

10 August 1979

Īśvara Svarūpa, Deviji and I went to the city one day. He gave the keys to us, asking us to keep them as he would return after us. But he happened to go back earlier, while the keys were with us. He had no way to open the door, so he had to get in through a window. When we came back, he was furious and spared no words in scolding us. We just listened silently. Some of our relatives were present. Unable to see us berated thus, they got up and left. The next day we were invited to a place where those very relatives had also come. When they saw us sitting happily with Swamiji, they were so surprised and moved that tears were in their eyes. Watching them, Deviji sweetly said: "We have become like breads being baked in an oven. In its furnace-like heat, we swell up, but once out of it, we cool down equally fast. That anger you saw is what helps our minds to ripen. So why shed tears? The angry outbursts of the *guru* touch us only outwardly, inwardly, it only does us good." Everyone was pleased at this.

15 August 1979

A woman came into the *āśrama* and began to establish herself close to Swamiji. Out of pity for her, he too gave her the liberty to do so. Many years passed before her real malicious nature was revealed when she began to set herself against Sharika Deviji. One day, in the presence of several people, she used abusive words for her. Everyone protested and asked her to desist. When Gopinath reported the matter to Deviji and asked her why she did not tick her off, she said: "Listen, when a dog bites someone's leg, people don't run after the dog, they attend to the injured leg instead. Similarly we should try and stay away from such people, it is no use scolding them — their nature will not change."

23 December 1979

One night Īśvara Svarūpa asked us both to sit in front of him and practise meditation. I asked diffidently: "Sir, you say that one should always keep one's mind fixed on a point. One can do that if there is complete silence, but how is it possible when there is conversation?" While he was only thinking for the answer, Deviji spoke up impulsively: "Doesn't one engage in conversation sometimes while the mind is thinking of entirely different things? In the same way, one can talk while our gaze stays fixed inwards on our spiritual goal. That is what is meant by 'practising while conversing'."

20 March 1980

Deviji was sitting in a serious mood, when someone came and asked her: "There are some shallow-minded disciples in the *āśrama* who try to influence other disciples of Swamiji. Does their behaviour make them worthy?"

Deviji replied, in her gentle way: "Look, no one can become worthy merely by association, until he or she reforms his or her behaviour and actions. The fact that a great saint is smoking from it will not save the pipe of a *hookah* from turning sooty and black. The touch of his lips will not turn it white, it will always remain black. What effect will the saint have on it? In the same way, unless one's inner self is cleansed, Gurudeva can do nothing. *Śaktipāta* means the sudden, automatic transformation of one's nature."

26 June 1980

Swamiji was agonizing over some new disciples who had left the *āśrama*. Noticing his anxiety, Deviji observed: "It is hard to understand this behaviour of his. The higher a person rises on the spiritual plane, the arms of his actions are still pointed upwards, striving to rise even higher. It is strange that someone placed so high is letting his arms dangle downwards. Is it possible that a man like him will stretch his arms to such a low level? Which height is he occupying? Maybe he is only testing our faith by enacting a drama."

6 April 1981

We were taking a morning walk in the garden when I asked

Īśvara Svarūpa: "Work in the *āśrama* is increasing day-by-day. Daily chores hardly leave me any time to practise. I can't understand how you can maintain your detachment and retain *vimarśa*." Īśvara Svarūpa did not answer but Deviji quickly spoke up, *Śikhā dṛshyet cambare.*

"How is that an answer to my question?" I asked. "Svarūpaji has understood what I said."

Then Swamiji elaborated: "All the work done by one who has his mind fixed on the Absolute, is oriented towards the spiritual, just as a log keeps burning, but the light of its flame is always rising skywards." Deviji explained further: "You and the other material beings are like that log of wood, and keeping your minds fixed is like the flame which must keep aiming at the sky. That is how even while seemingly busy in daily material business, Gurudeva always stays detached. That is how you too should be."

12 April 1981

It was morning and the three of us were seated in the veranda, when Bruce Pollock came to collect his milk. When he saw Īśvara Svarūpa, he too sat down and an easy conversation on spiritual matters followed. Bruce said: "We practise so hard, keeping our minds alert, but don't seem to find any success. If it goes on like this, how shall we ever find self-realization? This method of practice seems like an endless exercise, with no respite at all. Shouldn't we follow some other path so that we reach the goal of self-realization?" Īśvara Svarūpa heard him patiently and then answered his query with an analogy.

> Once there were three farmers whose cultivations suffered because there had been no rain in their village. One day some one came and advised them to dig a well to save their crops. The first two farmers started digging, but only finding stones after some depth, started on another place and then another and another, finally discouraged, they gave up. The

> third was wiser than them. He started digging and persisted at that one spot, removing the stones and digging on till water was sighted. Delighted, he was able at last to irrigate his fields. The same applies to spiritual practice too. If you fix your mind with full faith and keep practising constantly, you are sure to find the fruit of your labour. Even if nothing else happens, you will still find peace of mind through such concentration. Success on the spiritual path cannot be achieved through mere argument, nor must you fall into worry. Stay happy and watch this playfulness of God, while immersing yourself in practice. This is the key to God-realization.

Listening to this elaboration, Bruce bowed his head before Guruji and then left.

13 April 1981

The next morning Bruce came again and sat with us, talking about spiritual matters. Īśvara Svarūpa asked him: "Why do you look sad?"

"When I am unable to reach my goal, how can I look happy and not be sad?" said Bruce. Īśvara Svarūpa answered: "You think your dejected look will impress God? This is no way to seek Him. It is as if the snake has gone into his hole and a fool plugs it with earth, imagining that the snake has been killed. But the snake is still inside, alive and content. Just brooding sadly is like plugging the snake's hole. Unless you practise with concentration, you cannot find God. Dejection will not help in your desire to find God. Always remain fixed on God with faith and devotion and He will surely reward your efforts."

15 April 1981

Īśvara Svarūpa had called a visitor for a lesson early in the morning. When it was over and he was coming back, Deviji said to me: "Look, Gurudeva has put the setting agent into the milk for turning it into yoghurt, now let us wait and watch in which forthcoming incarnation of his it will be ready and the man will find release. After all, a lesson too is like a little bit of a setting agent which turns milk into yoghurt."

22 April 1981

The same day I said to Īśvara Svarūpa: "I too want to express my feelings on your birthday before the assembled gathering. If John can speak, why can't I?" He listened without comment, but Deviji spoke instead, "It is better to keep silent. The frogs on the shore make so much noise, while the crocodiles in the deep waters say nothing. They are already established in stillness, why should they speak?" I had nothing to say to this.

5 July 1981

We were all studying the *Parātrīśikā*, trying to understand the treatise. One gentleman had understood to some extent and he began to loudly propound his views on it. Everyone kept quiet and did not respond. When they had all left for their homes, Deviji said to Santramji: "Learning words by rote, without having comprehended their real meaning is like handling and taking care of inanimate objects like a chair or a table or even pots and pans. Here a person picks up words instead of material objects — what is the difference? Had they comprehended the concepts fully, they would not have bandied words like this."

10 July 1981

We had just finished the *Parātrīśikā* and the three of us were sitting in the compound, discussing the meaning of the treatise, when Deviji pointed towards me and asked: "What did you understand by the words, *tyaja dharmādharmam*? Do they really mean giving up the ideas of right and wrong, duty and behaviour? No, that is not what they mean. You must understand *tyaj* here to mean reaching that state where you do not need to give up these distinctions, they drop off by themselves. You do not need to do anything — when you reach that state, you will know it yourself." Īśvara Svarūpa nodded in agreement.

11 July 1981

One day Deviji explained in a state of excitement about the spiritual and material types of *havana*: "What is *havana* (offerings to the Lord)? It is simply doing your daily chores like getting up, eating, speaking, looking after things, while remaining conscious of His presence. Those are the true offerings. If a person keeps practising in this spirit, he or she will become a liberated soul in no time at all. Always remain aware, that is the key to spirituality."

13 July 1981

All three of us were sitting in the veranda in the morning, when I spoke up: "There is need to do hard penance to find God-realization, I think I will give up staying here on Sundays, If I stay away from contact with the crowds that come here, I will be able to remain inward-looking and shall soon find the vision of God." Before Deviji could reply, Īśvara Svarūpa spoke: "Keep practising with concentration, and you will have the desired experience." At this Deviji said: "This path is not like trying to catch straying chicks, that you will call out to them in their lingo and they will rush to you! Here you need the subtle call of the soul, and practise with concentration and real comprehension. Then you don't need to give up anything, what needs to be given up, falls off by itself." Īśvara Svarūpa asked Deviji: "What all have you given up?"

Deviji answered, "What did I ever acquire that I have to give up? Everything has fallen off in my case." Īśvara Svarūpa said: "Does it mean you are *jīvanmukta*?"

"Maybe not before you, but to myself I certainly am." Both of us laughed in happiness.

14 July 1981

It was Tuesday morning, Īśvara Svarūpa's Monday-vow-of-silence was over and Deviji and I had come into his room to greet him. Īśvara Svarūpa addressed Deviji, "Tomorrow we will teach the foreigners". Deviji said: "Yes, go on teaching them, how does it matter to us? In this case teaching thus is behaving like that hawker who sells oranges, calling out, 'come, buy oranges!', without tasting a single piece of the fruit himself. For him, the price he gets is the only fruit he is interested in. So is the case with those holy men or women, who are only busy teaching others, 'God exists! God exists!'. Caught in this exercise, the only fruit they keep getting is items of luxury like a car. If they could taste the immortal fruit of God-realization themselves, they would have no desire for material luxuries, but only stay immersed in the joy of that taste. Having reached that stage, whom or what would they teach then?" This analogy appealed to Īśvara Svarūpa and he was very happy. "You have given an excellent example", he said.

1. Some women devotees were talking to each other when one commented, "Swamiji is like Lord Śiva Himself, but many women devotees like to see in him their object of love". Deviji said: "Who can claim to be the spouse of Śiva? You have heard of Rādhā Rānī (queen) or Sītā Rānī (queen), but no one has ever heard of Pārvatī being given this title of 'Rānī'. Pārvatī is established at the same peak as Śiva is, therefore even though she is His spouse, her separate identity is always maintained."
2. A helper in the *āśrama* came to ask whether he should collect the sawdust lying in the yard. Deviji smiled and said: "After putting itself to such tortured penance

in the sawmill, does this poor thing still only remain sawdust?"

3. Mohanlalji, our brother, came to visit and found Īśvara Svarūpa in one of his fiery moods that day, sparing no one in his fury. Mohanlalji was shocked and dismayed. Taking Deviji aside, he asked her how she could live in this atmosphere. She calmly replied: "Don't worry about me, what harm can fire do to water?"
4. Dinanathji Ganju, a devotee, came to the *āśrama* one day, complaining of all that had gone wrong in his affairs, frequently punctuating his narrative with, "alas!". Deviji listened for some time and then said: "Why not say 'So what?' instead of 'Alas!'? You will see how much better you feel."
5. I came into the room and found that Deviji was lost in thought, a pile of unwashed clothes before her. I asked her why she was not in the kitchen, attending to her usual routine of cooking. She replied, "I would certainly have done so, but look at the reproachful way in which these clothes are looking at me! They want me to wash them before I do anything else". Taking the gentle hint, I collected the clothes and took them to wash.
6. One day while having dinner, I asked Deviji not to have yoghurt, because it could cause breathlessness. Deviji said: "What is so strange about it? Breath must come and go and naturally, it can pause sometimes too. With inhalation and exhalation of breath, there will be moments of pause, so why worry about it?"
7. One day I said to Deviji, rather sadly: "We had our own house and we sold it for no reason. Where can we sing our *bhajana*s in freedom now?" At this Deviji gently reprimanded me: "God has given such a house

in the form of this body with its beautiful roof of head, where could you find a better place to sing *bhajanas*? What do you need a house for? *Bhajanas* only need concentration and faith, not a house."

Note: Translated from Prabha Deviji's original Hindi into English by Neerja Mattoo.

Śārikā Devī: The Cosmic Mother
In The Śākta Tradition of Kashmir

Advaitavadini Kaul

Śiva and Śakti are the two aspects of supreme truth. Śiva is Absolute Power and Śakti the Infinite Cosmic Energy. Both are inseparable. For the realization of this truth the Śāstras have suggested various ways or paths. Amongst these, considerable attention has been paid to adopting the path of devotion. It is an undeniable fact that the sincere love and true devotion is the basis for the development of the sense of motherhood in a seeker. The Supreme Reality as Śiva becomes conceivable through the worship and favour of Śakti as Mother.

India has a long tradition of mother worship. Parā Śakti has been described as the cosmic mother by the Vedas, the Upaniṣads, the Tantras and the Purāṇas. Devī-Sūkta of *Ṛgveda* proves the pre-eminent position occupied by the divine creatrix. Ilā, Mahī and Dakṣiṇā are divine powers in their own right. Aditi is worshipped as the prime mover and the Gāyatrī is meditated upon by all followers of the Brāhmanic lore. The Tantras advocate Parā Śakti as the originator and the source of all that we see or perceive:

तव च का किल न स्तुतिरम्बिके! सकलशब्दमयी किल ते तनुः।
निखिलमूर्तिषु में भवदन्वयो मनसिजासु बहिःप्रसरासु च।।

इति विचिन्त्य शिवे! शमिताशिवे! जगति जातमयत्नवशादिदम्।
स्तुतिजपार्चनचिन्तनवर्जिता न खलु काचन कालकलास्ति मे।।

tava ca kā kila na stutirambike! sakalaśabdamayī kila te tanuḥ ।
nikhila mūrtiśu me bhavadanvayo mansijāsu bahiḥ prasarāsu ca ॥
iti vicintya śive! śamitā śive! jagati jātamayatnavaśādidam ।
stuti japārcanacintana varjitā na khalu kācana kālakalāsti me ॥

— Abhinavagupta in *Śivaśaktyavinābhāvastotra* quoted in *Gītārthasaṁgraha* XV.19

O Pārvatī ! since Thou art the root of all speech, I may sing Thy glory or do otherwise, all that is an adoration to Thee.

Thou art present for me in all forms both mental and physical.

When I ponder over these thoughts, O Mother (consciousness), the doer of good and destroyer of evil!

Without any effort on my part thus passes all my time in singing Thy glory, in repeating Thy name, in adoring Thee and in meditation on Thy True Self . . .

— tr. Pandit Jankinath Kaul 'Kamal'

As the divine mother she creates, sustains and dissolves this universe. Through her compassion all creation — existent or non-existent comes into being. Therefore, cosmic mother is represented through each and every form perceivable in the mundane world. These representations are full of truth and mystery.[1]

Śārikā is one such representation unique to the Śākta tradition of Kashmir. As the presiding deity of the Pradyumna Pīṭha, Śārikā has been invoked and worshipped in the beautiful valley of Kashmir for centuries. Etymologically the word *śārikā*

---

1 Ref. *Devī Saptaśatī*, *Bhavānīsahasranāmastuti* and *Lalitā Sahasranāma* (*śata* and *sahasra* here represent infinite number).

is believed to be derived from the root *sar* meaning "to move" and *ka* meaning "water". Therefore the meaning of the word *śārikā* is interpreted to be as "one that moves in water". There is a Purāṇic mythology behind this interpretation. Satīsar — the ancient name of Kashmir comes from Satī — an aspect of Mahāmāyā Durgā who was born as one of the daughters to Dakṣa Prajāpati. She married Śiva. After the marriage Dakṣa performed a *yajña,* no invitation was sent to Satī and Śiva. But, Satī against the consent of Śiva attends the performance at her father's palace. Reaching there she feels insulted and jumps into the sacrificial fire. Knowing this Śiva reaches there from Kailāsa. Her ashes are flown in the Satīsar by Śaṅkara himself. In this way Satī, in the form of the ashes remained floating on the water. It is further said that out of her love for Śaṅkara-Śiva, Mīnāvatī — the celebrated better-half of Himalaya, while bathing in the lake, saw the ashes floating in the form of water-grass. She called *sarika-sarika* (the substance floating on water) and got the grass in her hands. As it was ordained, in course of time she (Mīnāvatī) gave birth to a daughter. This daughter came to be known as Pārvatī and she later married Śiva. Pārvatī is believed to have taken the form of Śārikā Devī or Śārikā Bhagavatī in Kashmir.

Kashmir was a vast lake in former time. It is believed that today's Kaunasarnag also known as Viṣṇupāda (in the south) and Haramukūṭa Gaṅgā or Gaṅgabal (in the north) have been the two landing points. *Nīlamatapurāṇa* says[2] that Jalodbhava — a demon reared by the *nāgas* was creating constant havoc to the peaceful life in the region. For getting rid of him, Ṛṣi Kaśyapa prayed to Viṣṇu and Śiva. As a result of his prayers the lake was emptied and the demon's head was cut. But, the surviving *daityas* continued to create trouble for the inhabitants

2 *Nīlamtapurāṇa,* pp. 201-04, 227-28, 237-38ff.

by coming out through the water pool near Khushalsar situated in the centre of the present Srinagar city.

Another legend corroborating with this is taken from *Śārikā Māhātmya*[3] which relates that the Goddess Durgā taking the form of Śārikā ("Sārikā" meaning a particular bird called "Har" in Kashmiri) carried pebbles in her beak from the mount Meru and dropped them at the hole so that to stop the emersion of the *daitya*s. By this a hill arose at the place and subsequently the goddess made this hill her abode along with other *deva*s and *gaṇa*s around the hill to assure all inhabitants of her protection.

The hill came to be known as Śārikā Parvat or Hari Parvat or simply "Parbat" as we know the place in Kashmiri language. The goddess is worshipped and meditated upon here in the form of a sandy rock anointed with *sindūra* (red lead) and is believed to bear Śrīcakra[4] — the *saguṇa* form of Śrī Vidyā of the Śāktas. Thus, known as Cakreśvara (name of the place) or

---

[3] *Śārikā Māhātmya* (hereafter referred as *ŚM*) in *Bhṛṅgiśa Saṁhitā*:

ततस्तु सा महादेवी रूपं कृत्वा महीतले।
शारिकायास्तु तच्चञ्चु गृहीत्वा शृङ्गमुत्तमम्।।

तेन शृङ्गेन सा देवी भूमिरन्ध्रमपूरयत्।
रुद्धं तु गिरिणा द्वारं दृष्ट्वा दैत्यो बलेन हि।।

देवी क्रुद्धा जगन्माता शारिका स्वविभूतिभिः।
समन्तः शिखरे तस्यै सर्वदेवगणैः सह।।

tatastu sā mahādevī rūpaṁ kṛtvā mahītale ।
śārikāyāstu taccañcu gṛhītvā śṛṅgamuttamam ।।

tena śṛṅgena sā devī bhūmirandhramapūrayat ।
ruddhaṁ tu giriṇā dvāraṁ dṛṣṭvā daityo balena hi ।।

devī kruddhā jaganmātā śārikā svavibhūtibhiḥ ।
samantaḥ śikhare tasyai sarvadevagaṇai saha ।। — *ŚM* II.1-2, 4

[4] श्रीविद्यादर्शने लग्नो जपध्यानपरायणः।
यन्त्रेशपूजने सक्तो पश्येद्देवीमनुत्तमाम्।।

śrīvidyādarśane lagno japadhyāna parāyaṇaḥ ।
yantreśapujane sakto paśyeddevīmanuttamām ।। — *ŚM* V.40

Cakreśvarī (name of Devī) as well. This makes the place highly charged seat with spirituality (*siddha pīṭha*) also known as Pradyumna Pīṭha[5] — the place that shines from all sides by the intensity of the light of her (Śārikā's) grace.[6] Interpretations are given of the words *śārikā*, *pīṭha* and *pradyumna* in *Śārikā Māhātmya*.[7]

> *Śrīcakra* is a figure of symmetrical lines, esoterically representing beauty and harmony on which the eternal geometrician fashions the universe. Its centre is the source of all power and is represented by a point called *bindu*. Parā-Śakti resides in the triple *bindu* within the circle of infinity. In worshipping the form Śakti is praised as surrounded by *cakra-devatās*.[8]

The worship through *cakra* is more abstract. The Goddess Śārikā is also praised and contemplated upon as the most beautiful and magnificent deity with eighteen arms.[9] She is meditated upon with the recitation of the following verse:

---

5 a. तद्दुररक्षाहेतोश्च यत्र दुर्गं न्यवेशयत्।
आराध्य सा स्तुतिशतैः शारिकानामधारिणीम्।।
येन प्रद्युम्नशिखरं शारिकाकूटमित्यपि।
नामद्वयेन तत्तत्र स्थानमध्याभिधीयते।।

taddvurarakṣāhetośca yatra durgaṁ nyaveśayat ।
ārādhya sā stutiśataiḥ śārikānāmadhāriṇīm ॥
yena pradyumnaśikharaṁ śārikākūṭamityapi ।
nāmadvayena tattatra sthānamadyābhidhīyate ॥

— Somadeva, *Kathāsaritasāgara*, 12.6.110-11

b. *Pradyumnaksitidharanibha* . . . — *Vikramāṅkadevacarita* (18.15) of Bilhan (tenth century); also see for the name Pradyumna: Kalhan III.460, VII.1616; Srivara, *Zainarājataraṅginī*, I.7.105, II.88.

6 *tvattejasā samākrāntaṁ prakarṣaṁ dyotate tataḥ* ॥ – *ŚM* I.23 cd.

7 Ref. *ŚM* II.7-13.

8 Jankinath Kaul, 'Kamal', *Kashur Samachar*, July 1994, p. 24.

9 In *Svacchandabhairavatanta* (*ST*) Śakti is described by Kṣemarāja as →

अघोर व्याधिनाशी च घोर दुःख निवारिणी।
अष्टादशभुजादुर्गा शारिका श्यामसुन्दरी।।

aghora vyādhināśī ca ghora duḥkha nivāriṇī ।
aṣṭādaśabhujā durgā śārikā syāmasundarī ॥

All dynamism of consciousness appears in speech or language. This is also known as *vimarśa* (deliberation). All thinking gets its expression in language or in phonetics. Therefore Śakti is also known as *nāda* (sound), *vāk* (speech) and *śabda* (word). The source of *śabda* is Parā-Vāk that appears through the subtle and gross forms as *paśyantī, madhyamā* and *vaikharī*. The supreme power of Parā-Vāk or Parā-Śakti is known as *bindu*. In yogic parlance this is the *kuṇḍalinī śakti* in three-and-a-half coils giving rise to Jyeṣṭhā, Raudrī and Ambikā Śaktis as explained in the Tāntric tradition. These *śakti*s (energies) correspond to अ (supreme awareness), इ (unshaken will) and उ (unshaken knowledge). From these three vowel sounds arise eight (or nine) groups of speech as under:

1. Āmā or अवर्ग = अ–अः
2. Kāmā or कवर्ग = क–ङ
3. Carvāṅgī or चवर्ग = च–ञ
4. Ṭaṇkadhāriṇī or टवर्ग = ट–ण
5. Tārā or तवर्ग = त–न
6. Pārvatī or पवर्ग = प–म
7. Yakṣiṇī or यवर्ग = य–व
8. **Śārikā** or शवर्ग = श–ह
9. Kṣemaṅkarī क्ष त्र ज्ञ

→ forming eigtheen arms of Bhairava:

एकैकस्याश्च शक्तेस्त्रैरूप्यान्नवत्वम्, तत्रापि परापरभेदेन द्वैविध्यादष्टादशभुजत्वम्।

ekaikasyāśca śaktestrairūpyānnavatvam tatrāpi parāparabhedena dvaividyādaṣṭādaśabhujatvam — *ST*, vol. I, p. 54.

The eighth group of श ष स ह represents Ṣaḍ-vidyā, Īśvara, Sadāśiva and Śakti in the *vimarśa* (deliberation) aspect of Śiva. They are not created but are "the heat of His own nature". The *uṣmas* — as this group of letters is known in Sanskrit grammar. Therefore Śārikā — the heat given out — is expressed in the following five glories of Śiva-Śakti:

1. Sarvavyāpakatā (all-pervasiveness),
2. Pūrṇatā (all completenss),
3. Sarvajñatā (all knowingness),
4. Sarva-kartṛtā (all powerfulness), and
5. Nityatā (all existence).

This is the Cakreśvarī form of Śārikā in the Mātṛkā-cakra (the wheel of alphabets).[10]

In one of the verses of *Gaurī-Stotra* (*GS*) which is very popular amongst Kashmiris, Ādi Śaṅkara adores Mother Gaurī as:

आदिक्षान्तां अक्षरमूर्त्या विलसन्तीं
भूते भूते भूत-कदम्बं प्रसवित्रीम्।
शब्दब्रह्मानन्दमयीं तां प्रणवाख्यां।
गौरीं अम्बां अम्बुरुहाक्षीं अहं ईडे।।

ādikṣāntāṁ akṣaramūrtyā vilasantīṁ ।
bhūte bhūte bhūta kadambaṁ prasavitrīm ॥
śabda brahmānandamayīṁ tāṁ praṇavākhyāṁ ।
gaurīṁ ambāṁ amburuhākṣīṁ ahaṁ īḍe ॥ — *GS* 7

---

[10] Also ref. *ŚM* V.45:

एषा वाक्षररूपेण प्रादुर्भूता यदा हृदि।
निष्पथा च ततो देवी प्राह प्रश्रितया गिरा:।।

eṣā vākṣara rūpeṇa prādūrbhūtā yadā hṛdi ।
niṣpathā ca tato devī prāha praśritayā girā ॥

I propitiate the lotus-eyed, the universal mother who evolves through alphabetical formations from A to kṣa, who produces groups of creation — animate and inanimate — in the compositional process of the five elements; who is soundless sound of the universe and whose name, as explained by the Vedas, is *praṇava*, the three-syllabled *auṁ*.

— tr. Pt. Jankinath Kaul 'Kamal'

In the same context *Bhavānī-nāma-sahasra-stuti* describes the goddess as *śārikā śukabhāṣiṇī*[11] — one who like the bird sings melodious notes is 'Śārikā". Here Parā-Śakti is described as Śārikā — the power of indistinct note of melody in the states of *paśyantī* and *madhyamā*. This mental activity is known *vimarśa* — the Śakti Herself. And, when she appears in gross form then is known as *vaikharī* — the distinct spoken word.

Śārikā, her beatuy, bounty and benefaction have been expressed in beautiful verses throughout the tradition. These are mostly the *dhyāna ślokas* in Sanskrit. Some popular verses recited with submission and devotion are quoted as under:

बीजैः सप्तभिरूज्ज्वलाकृतिरसौ या सप्तसप्तिद्युतिः
सप्तर्षिप्रणताङ्घ्रिपङ्कजयुगा या सप्तलोकार्तिहृत्
काश्मीरप्रवरेशमध्यनगरीप्रद्युम्नपीठे स्थिता
देवीसप्तकसंयुता भगवती श्रीशारिका पातु नः।।

bījaiḥ saptabhirūjjvalākṛtirasau yā saptasapti dyutiḥ ।
saptarṣi praṇatāṅghri paṅkajayugā yā sapta lokārtihṛt ।।
kāśmīra pravareśa madhya nagarī pradyumnapīṭhesthitā ।।
devī saptakasaṁyutā bhagavatī śrīśārikā pātu naḥ ।।

Seated on Pradyumna *pīṭha* — the exalted kingly seat in the central city of Kashmir and surrounded by the seven deities (*matṛkās*) of her own semblence whose form is effulgent with the seven sacred formulae, who shines like the millions and

11 *Bhavānī-nāma-sahasra-stuti* — name no. 909, pp. 414-15.

millions of suns, whose blessed feet the seven sages seek for refuge (and) who removes the ills of the seven worlds — may that Goddess Śārikā vouchsafe grace to us all.

— tr. Pt. Jankinath Kaul 'Kamal'

Also:

आमा चैवतु कामा च चार्वङ्गी टङ्कधारिणी।
तारा च पार्वती चैवयाद्यक्षिणी शारिकाष्टमी।।

āmā caivatu kāmā ca carvāṅgī ṭaṅkadhāriṇī।
tārā ca pārvatī caivayādyakṣiṇī śārikāṣṭamī।।

By this verse eight names representing eight groups of the power of speech (as already noted above) are worshipped/invoked.

Another *mantra*:

प्रद्युम्नशिखरासीनां मातृचक्रोपशोभिताम्।
पीठेश्वरी शिलारूपां शारिकां प्रणमाम्यहम्।।

pradyumna śikharāsīnāṁ mātṛcakropaśobhitāṁ।
piṭheśvarīṁ śilārūpāṁ śārikā praṇamāmyaham।।

Residing on the peak of Pradyumna, adorning the *matṛkā cakra*, the goodess of the *pīṭha* in the form of *śilā* (hill) or rock, I pay my benedictions to Śārikā.

With the passage of time the prayers were composed also in local vernaculars as the spontaneous expressions or outpourings in Persian and Kashmiri. In later period we come to know of many *sādhaka*s in Kashmir who by receiving the blessings of Devī Śrī Śārikā have achieved higher stages of spiritual attainments. In day-to-day life some were blessed to have the goddess, in this mundane world living with them as their daughter. Pandit Madhavajoo Dhar received the blessings from the Goddess Śārikā taking birth as his daughter in the year 1621. She came to be known as Mātā Rūpa Bhavānī. Her *Rahasyopadeśa* is highly revered. In this context the following blessings to be received through the *pradakṣiṇā* of the Parbat is noteworthy:

> अर्धं वा पादशेषं वा परिक्रमति मण्डलम्।
> इह पुत्री सुखी भूत्वा सोऽन्ते याति परां गतिम्।।
>
> *ardhaṁ vā pādaśeṣaṁ vā parikramati maṇḍalam* ।
> *iha putrī sukhī bhūtvā so 'nte yāti parāṁ gatim* ॥
>
> — *ŚM* V.15
>
> One, who takes circumambulation of the remaining foot of the hill of this mountain, is blessed with daughter[12] and finally getting emancipated.

Likewise Pandit Jiya Lal Saraf has been totally devoted to Mother Śārikā. He has been a great *sādhaka* of the twentieth century. His Kashmiri translation of *Pañcastavī* is recited by all Kashmiris with full dedication and devotion to Mother Supreme. He has also composed other *stuti*s to Aṣṭādaśabhujā Śārikā which are dear to all mother worshippers. He practised *kuṇḍalinī yoga* and has composed a wonderful lullaby in which a mother initiates her son into the *kuṇḍalinī yoga*.

Bettina Bäumer, in February 2013 spoke to me about the forthcoming commemoration volume on Sushri Sharika Devi — the first disciple of Swami Lakshman Joo Mahārāj. She was a great Śaiva *yoginī*. Suddenly, it occurred to me that I had some time ago found a *Śārikā Stuti* composed in mixed Persian and Kashmiri. I thought that bringing it out in this volume along with a translation would be quite apt and Bäumer also agreed with this proposal.

It was Walter Slaje (Halle, Germany) who first drew my attention to this *stuti* in June 2004. He e-mailed a picture to me taken by him in the vicinity of Hari Parbat hill in September

---

12 Birth of a daughter has been considered a blessing. Thus the reference is also very important in the context of present-day problem of female foeticide.

2003, with a request to translate the lines written in Nastalikh script. I attempted the translation with the assistance of a Persian-knowing friend. This was it. But, in the second phase, while I was on a visit to my elder sister Nirmala Dhar in Jammu, I came across one of her notebooks, in which she had written down Kashmiri *stuti*s and *līlā*s in Devanāgarī script. There was a long *stuti* to Śrī Śārikā Devī in twenty-three stanzas. And, the stanza (no. 10) that I had attempted to translate earlier was from this *stuti*. I was thrilled to identify even the name of the author in this *stuti*. Pandit Krishnajoo Kar, about whom I had heard before, was a great devotee of Śrī Śārikā and a *sādhaka*. In the year 2006 when I visited Kashmir after a gap of eighteen years I got to visit the house of this *sādhaka* in Rainawari. I felt blessed. Another source has been *Kashur Samachar* magazine (August 1997, p. 68) in which the same *stuti* was published along with a translation in Hindi. But, it was not complete, only eleven stanzas were there. This was a chance identification in the back volumes of this community magazine, *Koshur Samachar*. I thought to myself that this *stuti* was fascinating; also for it being a specimen of a genre of literature representing a blend of Sanskrit, Persian and Kashmiri. I attempted editing this poem in order to get its meaning.

Pandit Krisnajoo Kar was one of the earnest devotees of Śrī Śārikā during the period of late seventeenth century. This was the period when Aurangzeb ruled India and Kashmir also came under his power. Pandit Krishnajoo Kar came from an affluent family and he was holding responsible post under the Mughals. At the same time he was also guiding many people on the spiritual path.[13] It is said that he used to visit

[13] Rishi Pīr and Misha Sab had received initiation from him. According to one information there was a painting in Pandit Krishnajoo Kar's house showing the trio together. However, no one knows what has been the fate of that historically important painting!

Mātā Śārikā Devī's *pīṭha* regularly, taking in one hand the earthen lamp and on the other some portion of meat for the offering. And Devī would accept his offerings always.

Paying my respects and adoration to Sushri Sharika Devi of Ishaber and the great disciple of Īśvara Svarūpa[14] Swami Lakshman Joo Mahārāj as a form of Śrī Śārikā Bhagavatī, my edited[15] and translated *stuti* composed by Pandit Krishnajoo Kar in praise of the goddess for invoking Her Blessings is presented below:

श्री शारिका देवी नमः

Obeisance to Goddess Śrī Śārikā
(*Ed. & Tr. Advaitavadini Kaul*)

वन्दे सरासर ईश्वरी श्री शारिका देवी नमः ।
मेहरे चराचर सुन्दरी श्री शारिका देवी नमः ॥

vande sarāsara īśvarī śrī śārikā devī namaḥ ।
mehare carācara sundarī srī śārikā devī namaḥ ॥

O Goddess personified! obeisance to (thee) Goddess Śrī Śārikā!
O gracious personified beauty! obeisance to (thee) Goddess Śrī Śārikā॥

अव्वल तुई आख़र तुई
हाज़िर तुई ज़ाहिर तुई

[14] It was Sushri Sharika Devi who addressed Swami Laksmanjoo Maharaj as Īśvara Svarūpa.

[15] I am thankful to Mansura Haider, Professor of medeival History, with whom I had several sittings for editing the text—heavily loaded with Persian words and expression. I have greatly enjoyed to edit and translate this *stuti*. It could not have been possible without the help of Mansura Haider's expertise.

गायब तुई बातिन तुई
श्री शारिका देवी नमः ॥ १ ॥

avvala tuī ākhara tuī
hāẓira tuī ẓāhira tuī
gāyaba tuī bātina tuī
śrī śārikā devī namaḥ ॥ 1 ॥

You are the beginning and the end (of this universe)
You are omnipresent and all-pervasive
You are both invisible and intrinsic
Obeisance to (thee) Goddess Śrī Śārikā ॥ 1 ॥

अज़ हर चे कारण बरतरे
दर हर दो आलम सरवरे
बर फ़रकि इन्दर अफ़सरे
श्री शारिका देवी नमः ॥ २ ॥

aẓa hara ce kāraṇa baratare
dara hara do ālama saravare
bara faraki indara afasare
śrī śārikā devī namaḥ ॥ 2 ॥

Whatever be the reason you are always supreme
You are omnipotent in both the worlds
You are the diadem of Indra's face
Obeisance to (thee) Goddess Śrī Śārikā ॥ 2 ॥

हर पंज कारण भक्ति तू
फ़रमा रवाये शक्ति तू
सर कर्द ज़ेरे तख्ते तू
श्री शारिका देवी नमः ॥ ३ ॥

hara pañja kāraṇa bhakti tū
farama ravāye śakti tū
sara karda zere takhte tū
śrī śārikā devī namaḥ ॥ 3 ॥

All five elements fructify in devotion to you
Your power maintains the order (of this universe)
I place my head under your throne
Obeisance to (thee) Goddess Śrī Śārikā ॥ 3॥

लछमी (लक्ष्मी) जहां आराए तू
माया विशन अफ़ज़ाए तू
बुद्धी महा विद्या तुई
श्री शारिका देवी नमः ॥ ४ ॥

lachamī (lakṣmī) jahāṅ ārāe tū
māyā viśana afaẓāe tū
buddhī mahā vidyā tuī
śrī śārikā devī namaḥ ॥ 4 ॥

As the goddess of wealth you adorn the entire universe
You are the extension of the play of Viṣṇu
You are the wisdom and the knowledge supreme
Obeisance to (thee) Goddess Śrī Śārikā ॥ 4 ॥

नूरे जहांने दावरे
ता बन्दा मेहरे अनवरे
माहे फ़िरोज़ां अख्तरे
श्री शारिका देवी नमः ॥ ५ ॥

nūre jahāṅne dāvare
tā bandā mehare anavare
māhe firoẓāṅ akhtare
śrī śārikā devī namaḥ ॥ 5 ॥

Your light encompasses the whole universe (like) —
The illuminating rays of sun,
The full moon and a bright star
Obeisance to (thee) Goddess Śrī Śārikā ॥ 5 ॥

सेहमो गुज़न्द फरवाह नत
शिव शक्ति जेरे आँ सनत

लालो जवाहिर दामनत
श्री शारिका देवी नमः ॥ ६ ॥

sehamo guẓanda faravāha nata
śiva śakti jere ām̐ sanata
lālo javāhira dāmanata
śrī śārikā devī namaḥ ॥ 6 ॥

Troublesome arrows are sublimed under your sovereignty
You are the evidence of Śiva's Śakti
All precious rubies and diamonds are in your lap
Obeisance to (thee) Goddess Śrī Śārikā ॥ 6 ॥

सीमो ज़रे बहरे दुरे
लालाए लाला गौहरे
ज़ेबे दो आलम सरवरे
श्री शारिका देवी नमः ॥ ७ ॥

sīmo ẓare bahare dure
lālāe lālā gauhare
zebe do ālama saravare
śrī śārikā devī namaḥ ॥ 7 ॥

All silver and gold are but for your ear-ornaments
Studded with rubies and pearls are your ornaments
You are the adornment of both the worlds
Obeisance to (thee) Goddess Śrī Śārikā ॥ 7 ॥

शक्ती तू कदरे शुद अयां
(शक्ति तू दर कुदरत अयां)
भक्ति तू मुक्ति जाविदां
तख्ते तु अरशे ला मकाँ
श्री शारिका देवी नमः ॥ ८ ॥

śaktī tū kadare śud ayāṅ
(śakti tū dar kudarat ayāṅ)
bhakti tū mukti jāvidāṅ

takhte tū araśe la makām̐
śrī śārikā devī namaḥ ॥ 8 ॥

Your power is perceived through this natural phenomenon
Devotion to thee is the source of permanent emancipation
Your place is extended to the entire sky
Obeisance to (thee) Goddess Śrī Śārikā ॥ 8 ॥

गर्दे रहत कामिल बसर
खाके दरत नूरे क़मर
संगे समीरत किश्ते ज़र
श्री शारिका देवी नमः ॥ ९ ॥

garde rahata kāmila basara
khāke darat nūre qamar
saṅge samīrat kiśte ẓar
śrī śārikā devī namaḥ ॥ 9 ॥

The dust of your path provides complete vision (as)
The dust of your seat shines like the rays of moon
The stone of your *sumeru* produces gold
Obeisance to (thee) Goddess Śrī Śārikā ॥ 9 ॥

चक्रीश्वर हाजत रवा
साज़द गदा रा बादशा
वाह वाह छ्यु लछमी थापना
श्री शारिका देवी नमः ॥ १० ॥

cakrīśvara hājata ravā
sāẓada gadā rā bādaśā
vāha vāha chyu lachamī thāpanā
śrī śārikā devī namaḥ ॥ 10 ॥

Cakreśvara fulfils the desires of all
(This highly charged seat) makes a beggar the king

Wow! how luxurious is this seat
Obeisance to (thee) Goddess Śrī Śārikā ॥ 10 ॥

देवी जगत्माता तुई
शिव शक्ति गोर दाता तुई
माता पिता भ्राता तुई
श्री शारिका देवी नमः ॥ ११ ॥

devī jagatmātā tuī
śiva śakti gora dātā tuī
mātā pitā bhrātā tuī
śrī śārikā devī namaḥ ॥ 11 ॥

O Devī! you are the mother of the entire universe
You are Śiva-Śakti, the guru and the giver (of everything)
You are the mother, father and brother
Obeisance to (thee) Goddess Śrī Śārikā ॥ 11 ॥

हाजत रवाए आलमे
शाहे जहांने अक्रमे
काइम मुकामे दाएमे
श्री शारिका देवी नमः ॥ १२ ॥

hājat ravāe ālame
śāhe jahāṅne akrame
kāim mukāme dāeme
śrī śārikā devī namaḥ ॥ 12 ॥

You are the one fulfilling the wish of all
You are the most beneficent ruler of the entire world
You are the permanent successor of eternity
Obeisance to (thee) Goddess Śrī Śārikā ॥ 12 ॥

मन अज़ तू नाढ़ी चक्रिमन
ध्यान अज़ ज़पा मालाइ मन
प्राण अज़ तु प्राणायामि मन
श्री शारिका देवी नमः ॥ १३ ॥

mana az tū nāḍhī cakriman
dhyāna az ẓapā mālāi man
prāṇa az tu prāṇāyāmi man
śrī śārikā devī namaḥ ॥ 13 ॥

My mind is but your *nāḍī cakra* (engaged in awakening *kuṇḍalinī*)
I meditate on the rosary of your names
My life-breath is in the mental recitation of your names
Obeisance to (thee) Goddess Śrī Śārikā ॥ 13 ॥

मन अर्स जोयम बे नवा
उफ्ताद अंबे दस्ते ता
दस्तम बिगीर अज़ तू दया
श्री शारिका देवी नमः ॥ १४ ॥

mana arsa joyam be navā
uftāda aṁbe daste tā
dastam bigīr aẓa tu dayā
śrī śārikā devī namaḥ ॥ 14 ॥

Small and poor fellow as I am in search for something big
O mother! I am falling in your hands
Out of mercy — kindly hold my hand
Obeisance to (thee) Goddess Śrī Śārikā ॥ 14 ॥

तू चार दह रत्ने गरां
तू नव निधाने जाविदां
तू काने गौहर दुर अमां
श्री शारिका देवी नमः ॥ १५ ॥

tū cār dah ratne garāṅ
tū nava nidhāne jāvidāṅ
tū kāne gauhar dur amāṅ
śrī śārikā devī namaḥ ॥ 15 ॥

You are the heavenly fourteenth jewel[16]
You are the inexhaustible treasure (*nava-nidhāna*)[17]
You are the mine of pearls (which are) like the
protective ear-rings[18]
Obeisance to (thee) Goddess Śrī Śārikā ॥ 15 ॥

उस्तादि माजिर नशितपीर
दर बन्दे गम गश्ते असीर
अज़ हातिफ़े दस्तंबिगीर
श्री शारिका देवी नमः ॥ १६ ॥

ustādi mājir naśtipīr
dar bande gam gaśte asīr
aẓa hātife dastaṁbigīr
śrī śārikā devī namaḥ ॥ 16 ॥

I am a devastated and aged — speaking aloud
I have become captive in the prison of sorrows
Kindly send a messenger of good news
O preserver of this universe hold my hand!
Obeisance to (thee) Goddess Śrī Śārikā ॥ 16 ॥

अज़ खुद शुदम बेज़ारतर
दर बन्दे गम बेज़ारतर
बर हालि ज़ारे कुन नज़र
श्री शारिका देवी नमः ॥ १७ ॥

aẓa khud śudam beẓāratar
dar bande gam beẓāratar

16 Ref. fourteen jewels that came out of *samudra-manthana.*

17 Ref. the nine inexhausting treasures of Kubera:

महापद्मश्च पद्मश्च शङ्खो मकरकच्छपौ।
मुकुन्दकुन्दनीलाश्च सर्वश्च निधयो नव॥

18 Putting in ear-rings to safeguard human beings has been practised since ancient times.

bar hāli ẓāre kun naẓar
śrī śārikā devī namaḥ || 17 ||

I am disenchanted with myself
Sorrows have imprisoned me
Kindly have mercy on my pathetic condition
Obeisance to (thee) Goddess Śrī Śārikā || 17 ||

दर बख्ते खुद अजदाद कुन
अज़ शाहेमन दिलशाद कुन
मूक्षी दिहो आज़ाद कुन
श्री शारिका देवी नमः || १८ ||

dara bakhte khud ajadād kun
aẓ śāheman dilaśād kun
mūkṣī diho āẓād kun
śrī śārikā devī namaḥ || 18 ||

Bestow upon me something from your great fortune
Kindly make me happy through my Lord
Provide me a permanent emancipation through deliverance
Obeisance to (thee) Goddess Śrī Śārikā || 18 ||

करदम दिले दर ज़ोकि तू
मादाम ख्वाहम शीशे तू
शौक़े तु फ़ौके ज़ौके तू
श्री शारिका देवी नमः || १९ ||

karadam dile dar ẓoki tū
mādāma khvāham śīśe tū
śauke tu fauke ẓauke tū
śrī śārikā devī namaḥ || 19 ||

I am aiming my heart on you
Perpetually I long for you

My yearning for your face adds to the lustre of my
love for you
Obeisance to (thee) Goddess Śrī Śārikā ॥ 19 ॥

रोगन चरागे पाम्पुरी
सिन्दूर खासे लोहुरी
चेहरत कुनम ज़र (ज़री) रोजरी
श्री शारिका देवी नमः ॥ २० ॥

rogan carāge pāmpurī
sindūra khāse lohurī
ceharata kunam ẓara (ẓarī) rojarī
śrī śārikā devī namaḥ ॥ 20 ॥

With the clarified butter from Pampore for the lamps
(And with) special *kumkum* (*sindūra*) from Lahore (and)
The brocade from Rajauri I adorn thee
Obeisance to (thee) Goddess Śrī Śārikā ॥ 20 ॥

गुल अज़ सरे खुद मी कुनम
ब्रिज अज़ दिलो जां आवुरम
पूज़ाइ तू ख्वाहम कुनम
श्री शारिका देवी नमः ॥ २१ ॥

gul aẓ sare khud mī kunam
brija aẓ dilo jāṅ āvurama
puẓāi tū khvāham kunam
śrī śārikā devī namaḥ ॥ 21 ॥

I am confronting my mind
My heart and soul want to bring in Braja[19]

19 If I understand it rightly the poet-devotee goes to the extent of expressing his own oneness with the goddess just like Rādhā — the queen of Braja who is one with her Lord Kr̥ṣṇa — and here Kr̥ṣṇa is the name of the poet-devotee as well. That is a reason for confrontation.

(And) continue to worship you
Obeisance to (thee) Goddess Śrī Śārikā ॥ 21 ॥

हर सुब्ह दम गोयम तुता
हर रोज़ शब अज़ तू क्रिया
बर अस्ल नसलम कुन दया
श्री शारिका देवी नमः ॥ २२ ॥

har subha dam goyam tutā
har roza śab aẓ tū kriyā
bara asla nasalam kun dayā
śrī śārikā devī namaḥ ॥ 22 ॥

Every morning I praise you
The turn of night and the day takes place through your creation
Kindly have mercy upon all my near and dear ones
Obeisance to (thee) Goddess Śrī Śārikā ॥ 22 ॥

ही इष्ट देवी शारिका
दासी तु केहतर कृष्णकार
गोयम तोता जोयम दया
श्री शारिका देवी नमः ॥२३ ॥

hī iṣṭa devī śārikā
dāsī tu kehatar kṛṣṇakār
goyam totā joyam dayā
śrī śārikā devī namaḥ ॥ 23 ॥

O my presiding deity
I Kṛṣṇakār, the meanest of mean servants
Utter the praises and seek your compassion
Obeisance to (thee) Goddess Śrī Śārikā ॥ 23 ॥

Plate 1: Devī (specimen of paintings distibuted by family priests among children specifically on Gaurī Tritīyā day to invoke goddess of learing) (Photo: Kapil Kaul)

Plate 2: Śāradā Devī: Painting by Pandit Narayan Murchagar (Photo: Kapil Kaul)

Plate 3: On the way to Pradyumna Pitha in Devi Angan, the arch has lines from Pt. Krishnajoo Kar's *Devī-Stuti* in Persian language (Photo: Walter Slaje)

Plate 4: A view of Sarika Parvata — Hari Parbat (Photo: Walter Slaje)

Plate 5: Śārikā Śila with Śrīcakra-Cakreśvarī (Photo: Walter Slaje)

Plate 6: Aṣṭādaśabhujā Śārikā

Plate 7: Ruins of Pandit Krishnajoo Kar's house in Rainawari as seen in October 2006

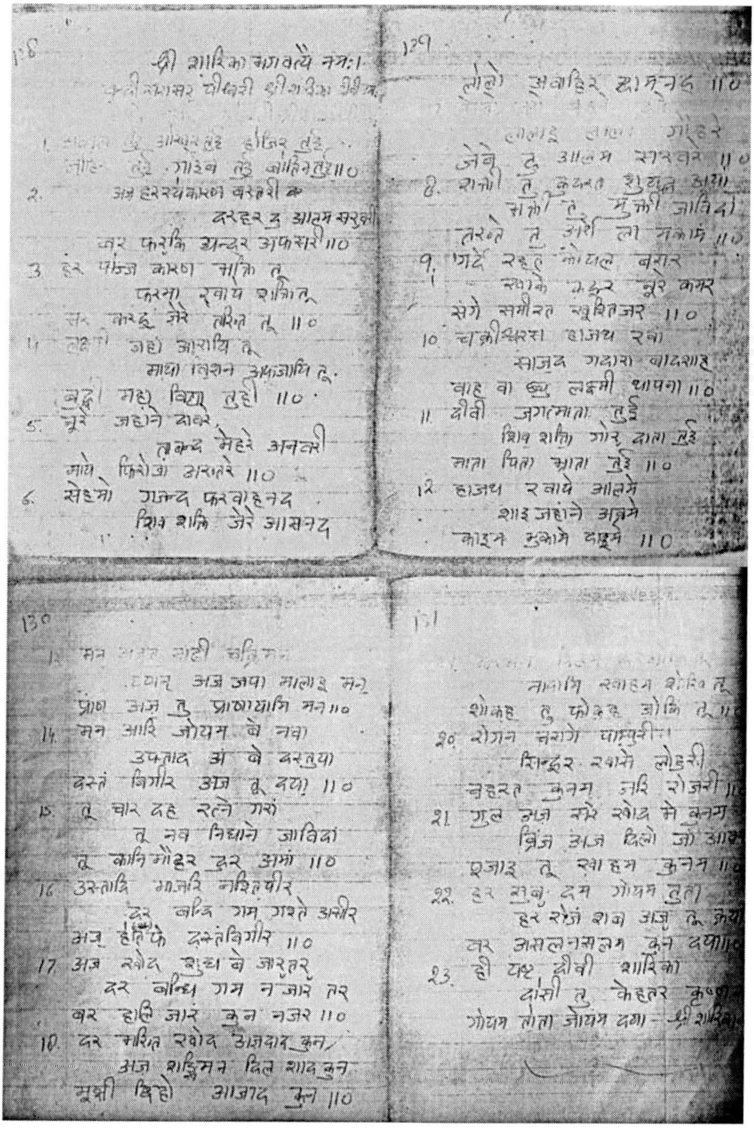

Plate 8: Manuscript of Pt. Krishnajoo Kar's *Śārikā-Stuti*

Bibliography

Bhatta, Somadeva, *Kathāsaritsāgara*, ed. Pandit Durgaprasad and Asinath Pandurang, revised by Vasudev Laxman Sastri Pansikar, Bombay: Nirnayasagar Press, 1930.

Dhar, Kashnath (tr.), *Srivara's Jaina Rājataraṅginī*, New Delhi: Indian Council of Historical Research and People's Publishing House, 1994.

'Kamal', Jankinath Kaul, *Pañcastavī* (*the Pentad of Hymns of Kuṇḍalinīyoga*), Srinagar: Sri Ramakrishna Ashrama, 2001 (2nd edn.).

——— (tr. & com.), *Bhavānī-nāma-sahasra-stuti* (*The Thousand Names of Bhavānī*): *A Page from Rudrayāmala Tantra*, Srinagar: Sri Ramakrishna Ashrama, 1991.

——— (ed. & com.), *Mukundamālā evaṁ anya stotra-ratna* (in Hindi) Cūḍāmaṇi Granthamālā-1, 1994 (3rd edn.).

——— "The Eighteen-Armed Goddess Sharika: Cultural and Spiritual Aspect", *Koshur Samachar*, New Delhi: Kashmiri Samiti, July 1994, pp. 23-2[illegible]

Kar, Sriyut K[illegible]ajoo "Śri Śārikā Devī Namaḥ", in *Kashur Samachar*, New Delhi: Ka[illegible]hmiri Samiti, August 1997, p. 68.

Khajuriya, Yashpal (ed.), "Śārikā Mā[illegible]ātmya", in *Bhṛṅgīśa Saṁhitā* (*Topography of Ancient Kashmir*), Jam[illegible] Sri Ranvir Kendriya Sanskrit Vidyapitha, 1985.

Kumari, Ved, *The Nīlamata Purāṇa*, vol. II, Srinagar: Jammu and Kashmir Academy of Art Culture and Languages, 1994 (2nd edn.).

Pandey, Sri Ramnarayandatt Shastri, 'Ram' (tr.), *Śrīdurgā Saptaśatī*, Gorakhpur: Gita Press, Saṁvat 2047 (repr.).

Shastri, Madhusudan Kaul (ed.), *Svacchandatantra with Uddyota of Ksemara[illegible]* vol. I, Delhi: Sanskrit Gian Sansthan, 1986 (repr.).

Śrī Lalitā Sahasranāma, with *nāmāvalī*, Chennai: Giri Trading Agency, [illegible]05 (repr.).

Stein, M.A., *Kalhaṇa's Rājataraṅgiṇī*, in 3 vols., Delhi: Motilal Banarsidass, 1989 (repr.).